THINK
ABUNDANCE

Dr. Norman Thomas Jr.

Unless otherwise noted, all scripture is from the New King James Version of the Bible.

Scripture quotations mark *Amplified Bible, Classic Edition*, are taken from the Amplified Bible. Copyright © 1954, 1958, 1962, 1964, 1965, 1987, 2015 by The Lockman Foundation. Used by permission.

Scripture quotations marked *The Message* are taken from The Message, copyright © 1993, 1994, 1995, 1996, 2000, 2001, 2002. Used by permission of NavPress. All rights reserved. Represented by Tyndale House Publishers, Inc.

Scripture quotations marked *New Living Translation* are taken from the Holy Bible, New Living Translation, copyright © 1996, 2004, 2007, 2013 by Tyndale House Foundation. Used by permission of Tyndale House Publishers Inc., Carol Stream, IL 60188. All rights reserved.

Scripture quotations marked *New International Reader's Version* are taken from the Holy Bible, New International Reader's Version®, NIRV® Copyright © 1995, 1996, 1998, 2014 by Biblica, Inc.™ Used by permission of Zondervan.

Scripture quotations marked *New International Version* are taken from the Holy Bible, New International Version®, NIV® Copyright ©1973, 1978, 1984, 2011 by Biblica, Inc.® Used by permission. All rights reserved worldwide.

Think Abundance
By Dr. Norman Thomas, Jr.

©2018 by Dr. Norman Thomas, Jr.

ISBN: 978-1-7327062-0-0

Published by Norman Thomas Ministries | 3000 East Gauthier Road, Lake Charles, LA | www.NormanThomas.org

Editorial by Jordan Media Services | P.O. Box 761593 | Fort Worth, Texas USA | www.jordanmediaservices.com

Typesetting/Layout by Ken Fraser | www.impactbookdesigns.com

Printed in the United States of America. All rights reserved under International Copyright Law. No part of this book may be reproduced or transmitted in any form or by any means, electronic or mechanical, including photocopying, recording, or by any information storage and retrieval system, without the written permission of the publisher.

Contents

Introduction..5

Chapter 1 | Faith for Abundance................................7

Chapter 2 | Abundance: The Outcome of Seed Sown..........19

Chapter 3 | Abundance God's Way.............................30

Chapter 4 | Why Think Abundance?............................38

Chapter 5 | The Practicality of Abundance Thinking.............43

Chapter 6 | Abundance Is a Revelation........................49

Chapter 7 | Abundance Is a Mindset 59

Chapter 8 | The Place of Abundance..........................66

Chapter 9 | The Supernatural Nature of Abundance...........73

Chapter 10 | The Law of Attraction............................80

Introduction

The thief does not come except to steal, and to kill, and to destroy. I have come that they may have life, and that they may have it more abundantly.
—**John 10:10**

Ever since the fall of Adam and Eve from the Garden of Eden, provision has been mankind's greatest quest. Before that, things were different. When God created man in His image and after His likeness, He also provided for him unquestionable abundance. Abundance was the nature of the Garden, because abundance is the nature of God (Ephesians 3:20). Abundance served Adam, and his wife Eve, and whatever they needed was available at their command.

Since that time, mankind has had a problem discerning and accessing the abundant supply of the Father. Today, you and I have the privilege and opportunity to embrace God's gift of redemption through Jesus, which includes the inheritance of an inexhaustible, abundant supply of all things needed to complete our assignment on the earth, for as long as we live (2 Peter 1:3). There is truly nothing missing and nothing lacking in our lives.

Our access to this provision has been restored. But to enjoy the benefits of this inheritance, we must become knowledgeable of the kingdom of God and embrace the rules of engagement that governs it. Once this happens, the abundant supply of the Father's goodness will flow freely into our lives.

Chapter One

Faith for Abundance

Everything you will ever need for your life and your God-given assignment has already been provided. It has been that way since the beginning of time. Of course, that provision was forfeited for a time because of Adam and Eve's transgression in the Garden of Eden. They violated the one command that guaranteed their prosperity—that they would never have to want for anything—ever! Let's look at it in Genesis 2:15-17, *Amplified Bible, Classic Edition:*

> And the Lord God took the man and put him in the Garden of Eden to tend and guard *and* keep it. And the Lord God commanded the man, saying, You may freely eat of every tree of the garden; But of the tree of the knowledge of good and evil *and* blessing and calamity you shall not eat, for in the day that you eat of it you shall surely die.

It is apparent from this passage that it has never been God's intent for man to struggle and toil for provision and survival because of lack. Everything Adam and Eve needed was in the Garden. There was never a need to go outside the Garden for anything. In the same fashion, everything you need is in God's kingdom. There is never a need for you to venture outside His kingdom for anything. All Adam and Eve had to do was operate by the rules of garden living. But in Genesis 3:1-3 we find the beginnings of an event that would forever change the course of God's plan for humanity until the coming of Christ. The culture of the garden was violated. In the same way in which the serpent invaded the garden, the enemy invades the lives of people today through their thoughts—proposing doubt, fear, and unbelief regarding anything God has said.

Abundance Restored!

God's original plan for mankind was and remains a beautiful one. His plan has not changed. He sent Jesus as the "last Adam" (1 Corinthians 15:45) in order that He might once and for all redeem and restore humanity back to the quality of life that God intended for us from the beginning of time.

Toil is the inevitable outcome of choosing outside God's plan for your life and each time we do, we enter struggle and survival mode.

> He told the Man: "Because you listened to your wife and ate from the tree that I commanded you not to eat from, 'Don't eat from this tree,' the very ground is cursed because of you; getting food from the ground will be as painful as having babies is for your wife; you'll be working in pain all your life long. The ground will sprout thorns and weeds, you'll get your food the hard way, planting and tilling and harvesting, sweating in the fields from dawn to dusk, until you return to that ground yourself, dead and buried; you started out as dirt, you'll end up dirt" (Genesis 3:17-19, *The Message)*.

This was Adam and Eve's verdict once they opted out of God's plan for their lives. Toil has now become a way of life being passed on for generations to come. Notice how their choice resulted in their expulsion from the Garden—the place of their purpose, provision, and fellowship with the Father:

So, God expelled them from the Garden of Eden and sent them to work the ground, the same dirt out of which they'd been made. He threw them out of the garden and stationed angel-cherubim and a revolving sword of fire east of it, guarding the path to the Tree-of-Life (Genesis 3:23-24, *The Message*).

Jesus (the last Adam) came into the world as The Gift of the Father to humanity. Jesus, The Gift, comes with revelation and restoration of all that was lost before the Fall. He served as God's way of bringing us back to "Garden status." He paid the price of inheritance with His blood and redeemed us as His joint-heirs. Now that this price has been fully paid, we have the right to have and enjoy life, and have it "in abundance [to the full, till it overflows]" (John 10:10, *Amplified Bible, Classic Edition*).

Notice the word abundance. In its simplest form, *abundance* means "an extremely plentiful or over-sufficient quantity or supply." That's what Jesus said He came to bring to all mankind. An "extremely plentiful" supply and an "over-sufficient quantity" of all things needed for life and godliness. In other words, Jesus has already provided for us in every way possible. He's given us more than enough! The problem we have is our limited ability to recognize and perceive our supply. When Jesus hung on the cross, shed His blood, and died, He took upon Himself the poverty and lack of humanity, and in exchange He generously released the riches of heaven to us. He traded His abundance for our poverty in all things, spiritual and material.

"For ye know the grace of our Lord Jesus Christ, that, though he was rich, yet for your sakes he became poor, that ye through his poverty might be rich." —2 Corinthians 8:9

It's the same provision God made in the beginning of time when He placed Adam and Eve in the Garden.

No Stress Regarding Provision

Abundance! A word that many in the Body of Christ don't like hearing taught or preached, but because of its relationship to provision, we're thinking about it all the time. It's always on our minds! Abundance is the one thing that drives and mandates our focus and time in a dimension where provision is in such high demand.

Whether it's monthly bills, food, healthcare, tuition, retirement—the truth is, it's inevitable that most people are thinking about the abundance of provision, however subliminal it may be. Our lives are wrapped around what we perceive our needs, wants, and desires to be. Most people worry, or at least preoccupy their thoughts, with how these things are going to be taken care of. But based on Matthew 6, we can conclude that worry and anxiety are not part of God's strategy for getting our needs met.

In Matthew 6:25, *Amplified Bible, Classic Edition,* Jesus told His disciples, "Therefore I tell you, stop being perpetually uneasy (anxious and worried) about your life, what you shall eat *or what you shall drink*; or about your body, what you shall put on. Is not life greater [in quality] than food, and the body [far above and more excellent] than clothing?" Jesus makes this statement to men who had industrious, professional, and business backgrounds. He teaches them that it is the explicit plan of the Father to be their ultimate Provider and only Source and that it was never God's intent that we provide for ourselves (Matthew 6:26-27). This doesn't mean we don't work. It means that work is redefined for the believer. We now "seek first the Kingdom" (Matthew 6:33). In other words, we discover the assignment or the work of God for our lives. Instead of *job mentality,* we become highly developed in a *work mentality.*

Abundance Came With Jesus

In much the same way that He delivered the children of Israel and provided for them, God has already made provision for you and I today. He sent His Son to die for us and give us a life filled with abundance of provision and purpose, fullness of peace and joy, and an overflow of His favor toward us. Jesus died to redeem us from the curse, or the consequence of sin so we can live and be empowered by the Blessing. He became our atonement! Through Him, God has renewed His covenant with us, and He's abiding by that same covenant today in your life and mine. He says to us today the same words He spoke to His children in the days of old: "For I the Lord your God hold your right hand; I am the Lord, Who says to you, Fear not; I will help you!" (Isaiah 41:13).

Jesus reminds us that, "If God so clothe the grass of the field, which today is, and tomorrow is cast into the oven, *shall he not much more clothe* you?" (Matthew 6:30). Now it's up to us to take advantage of God's faithfulness to provide for us and receive the Blessing of His covenant. And it begins with developing faith in His Word of promise to provide. Unless we develop faith to embrace the truth concerning the abundance of God's provision, we will never enjoy the life He has planned, ordained, and purposed for us.

Many believers have grown up with a poverty mindset, thinking it is part of God's plan for them to be poor, never having been told that it's His will for them to prosper. They've been willing to settle for whatever came their way, convinced that the life of the believer was intended to be one of struggle and toil—striving on every hand to survive. But that's not what the Bible teaches. That image is so far removed from what God thinks and says about the care of His children. It bears no resemblance to what the Bible teaches about the nature of God and His provision and Blessing—that it's His will for us to prosper and be in health, even as our souls prosper (3 John 2).

It's important to recognize that abundance is not just about the accumulation of material things—about owning the biggest house on the block or driving the fanciest car.

Abundance is about living in God's best. It's about prospering in every area of life; first in spirit, soul and body. That can only happen when we "seek first the kingdom of God and His righteousness" (Matthew 6:33)—when we delight in His plans and purpose for our lives. When His agenda for us becomes our agenda, abundance will come to us.

Having a Proper Mindset

So, how do we get there? How do we pull ourselves up out of a place where a mindset of lack, shortage, or poverty has held us for so long, and make our way into the place where we can live in and enjoy God's abundance? It starts with our thinking. It begins with how we think and the reconciling of our thoughts with the Word of God. You see, if you're ever going to live the God-quality of life, if you're desiring to enjoy the abundance of the Blessing, you must change how and what you think regarding the concepts of lack and provision. By that, I mean you must take the courage to come into agreement with God as opposed to your experience, tradition, customs—even religion regarding His outlook on your life. As we said earlier, it was never God's intent for you to provide for yourself. He is your Father and He desires to provide for you fully. This doesn't mean you sit and do nothing. However, your job is not to "make provision" but rather to "believe" in the provision that has already been made for you by the Father. That provision comes in many forms, including supernatural abilities, wisdom, opportunities, and favor. These and many more streams will create a pathway for abundance to be added to you.

In Deuteronomy 8:17-18, *Amplified Bible, Classic Edition,* we read: "And beware lest you say in your [mind and] heart, My power and the might of my hand have gotten me this wealth. But you shall [earnestly] remember the Lord your God, for it is He Who gives you power to get wealth, that He may establish His covenant which He swore to your fathers, as it is this day."

Notice, there is a Source of abundance. That Source is God!

In this instance, He is providing wisdom through which abundance will come. In addition, abundance is purposed to "establish" or make tangible the promises of God's covenant. In God's view, there is no such thing as lack because in Him lack is illegitimate in all its forms. People only experience lack because they have been caused to see it as a reality. This is evident in Matthew 14, where Jesus fed well over five thousand people with only two fish and five loaves of bread.

Likely, you already know the story. The crowd had become increasingly tired and hungry after following Jesus for much of the day and listening to His teaching, when Jesus' disciples suggested He send them away, so they could return to their homes, eat, and rest. Their greater concern was that there was no way humanly possible to feed them all where they were and with their current level of resources at hand. And they were right. But the operative word here would be *humanly,* because Jesus had something else in mind that far exceeded anything the human mind could fathom. Read how that scene played out in Matthew 14: 15-21, *New International Version:*

As evening approached, the disciples came to him and said, "This is a remote place, and it's already getting late. Send the crowds away, so they can go to the villages and buy themselves some food." Jesus replied, "They do not need to go away. You give them something to eat."

"We have here only five loaves of bread and two fish," they answered. "Bring them here to me," he said.

And he directed the people to sit down on the grass. Taking the five loaves and the two fish and looking up to heaven, he gave thanks and broke the loaves. Then he gave them to the disciples, and the disciples gave them to the people. They all ate and were satisfied, and the disciples picked up twelve basketfuls of broken pieces that were left over. The number of those who ate was about five thousand men, besides women and children.

What took place that evening was supernatural, which resulted in overwhelming abundance. Jesus took five loaves of bread and two fish, empowered them by faith in the Blessing, and produced more than enough to feed 5,000 men, plus women and children. The pursuit of God's abundance will require you to engage the supernatural. It takes you off dependency on your senses, which is limited to engaging only the natural, three–dimensional reality.

A Closer Look at the Fall

I mentioned Adam and Eve and their transgression earlier. For just a moment, let's take a closer look at what was really going on with them back in the Garden. Before they disobeyed God's command, provision had never been a concern for Adam and Eve. Lack and insufficiency were never a consideration because abundance surrounded them. It served them.

Remember how the Garden was described in Genesis 2:8, *Amplified Bible, Classic Edition:* "And the Lord God planted a garden (*oasis*) in the east, in Eden (delight, land of happiness); and He put the man whom He had formed (created) there." The Bible calls it an *oasis* and a land of *happiness.* One definition of that word *oasis* is a place or location that "serves as a refuge, a source of relief, or pleasant change from what is ordinary, annoying, or difficult." They lived a life independent of conditions outside of the Garden. They had no need or lack needed or desired was available to them in the Garden.

That's why God planted the Garden first, then placed Adam and Eve there. He had always planned for their total provision. It wasn't until after the transgression, after they disobeyed God, that they lost their inheritance, including their rightful place in the Garden, and all the abundance of provision He had given them.

Although the enemy planned to sabotage God's original intent of good will toward man, his plan was thwarted by the coming of Jesus into the earth. He came as the 'life-giving Spirit' to restore all things and to make all things new (1 Corinthians 15:45). Jesus also came to destroy or undo all the work the devil had done (1 John 3:8). I refer to this as "reversing the verdict of the curse."

His assignment in the earth was and is to *dissolve* the curse that was brought into the earth by the enemy (John 10:10). The word *dissolve* is a powerful word. It's used to describe the word *destroy* in 1 John 3:8. As an English word, *dissolve* implies "a total dissipation, evaporation, and vanishing of a thing; to disappear." Once something is dissolved it cannot be put back together again. It cannot be restored to its original form or state. It literally melts away. So, once you came into Christ, you received the benefit of Jesus' work against all the works of the enemy in your life, including poverty, insufficiency, and lack. A major part of your redemption is abundance.

The problem with many believers today is that they're still living in the Adamic state. Although they are born again, they're still functioning at the level of fallen man—

willing to tolerate and pursue the world's way rather than the way of the Kingdom of God. This is because their minds are still connected to life according to the first Adam. But to live life according to the nature of the last Adam, Jesus, faith is required. A new way of thinking is mandatory! This is why the Apostle Paul was so insistent in his writings to suggest that we "put off the old man and put on the new man by the renewing of the spirit of our minds" (Ephesians 4:21-23).

Moving Forward In Faith

So, what's the solution? How do we position ourselves so that we're able to receive God's abundance—to live that abundant life Jesus spoke of? We find our answer in Matthew 6:33, where Jesus said: "But seek ye first the kingdom of God, and his righteousness; and all these things shall be added unto you."

What exactly are the "things" He's talking about? It's those things that will enable you to succeed, prosper and live victoriously in accordance with God's prescribed plan for you and your life. In Jeremiah 29:11, *The Message*, God makes a very profound statement about you and your life. He says: "I know what I'm doing. I have it all planned out—plans to take care of you, not abandon you, plans to give you the future you hope for." In other words, if you seek and follow God and not man, if you strive to live the way God desires for you to live—putting your faith, trust, and confidence in Him alone—then you will never have to want for anything. That is an amazing promise from our heavenly Father! Not only that, it's a promise He is more than willing and able to perform.

The reality of your life as a believer is this: Everything you will ever need has already been provided, planned, and prepared. Again, God never intended for you to have to provide for yourself. He had a plan for you, and the good news is He has never changed His mind about that plan.

Philippians 4:19, *Amplified Bible, Classic Edition,* says, "And my God will liberally supply (fill to the full) your every need according to His riches in glory in Christ Jesus." Notice it doesn't say *some* needs; it says *every* need. That word *every* covers a lot of territory. It covers your finances and your health. It covers family matters or a need for qualified employees. No matter what the need is, God says He's got it covered. And not only does He have it covered, but He said he will "liberally supply (fill to the full) your every need." Have you ever poured coffee in your cup until it overflowed? Or maybe you left the water running in the bathtub, not realizing it was at the point of being full, and it overflowed onto the bathroom floor? Why did it overflow? Because the water had no place else to go. It reached a saturation point, and nothing was in place to restrict the flow or hold it back. That's what's called *liberal supply*. It is supply in abundance to the point of flowing over. That's what God, through His Son, Jesus, has made available for each of us.

Chapter Two

Abundance: The Outcome of Seed Sown

How ridiculous would it be for a farmer to forego planting a crop, but at harvest time go out to his fields expecting to find a crop that is ready for harvesting? Or, what kind of sense would it make for someone who has never made a deposit of money into a bank, to one day show up at the bank expecting to make a withdrawal?

Quite honestly, both scenarios are laughable. In fact, both are ridiculous and make no sense at all. But the truth is, this type of thinking is more common than one might imagine. These scenarios speak directly to the mindset of many people, Christians included, who live their lives expecting to receive something when they've done nothing to position themselves to receive it. They're looking for, or expecting to receive God's abundance, but they haven't planted the seed of God's Word, including the practicing of Biblical principles that would position them to receive abundance.

There's nothing wrong with desiring, believing for or expecting abundance. But the truth is, it's senseless to have an expectation for something that you have not adequately prepared for—that you've not sown, or planted, a seed for. What do I mean by this? Before you build expectation to receive something, first invest in the development of faith that is necessary to access it.

As an employer, you would never feel obligated to pay any employee for work or services that were not rendered for your company. But once the seed of labor has been sown, the harvest of compensation can be reaped. When it comes to abundance, our seed of labor is believing and acting on the Word of God that references abundance. By this, I expand my spiritual capacity to properly manage God's abundance in my life.

Abundance, Not Accumulation!

Some people get abundance confused with accumulation. There is a difference. Actually, there's a BIG difference.

Accumulation is something most anyone can accomplish because it's a matter of logic and human effort. But abundance is spiritual and always the fruit of seed that has been sown. When you think of abundance from an agricultural perspective, for instance, it's impossible to have without giving just consideration to seed. Without the sowing of seed, nothing grows, and nothing is produced. If I refuse to plant the Word (spiritual seed) in my heart and become a giver (planting material seed into the lives of others) I have no right to expect that I should live in the abundance God has made available to me.

If I want apples, for instance, I can just go to the produce section of any grocery store and buy apples. But that's not abundance. That's just accumulation. All I've done is made a purchase of a preferred item. But when I've eaten all the apples I've purchased and desire more apples, I must go and purchase more.

On the other hand, if I have an apple tree in my backyard that I planted years ago, when a certain time of the year rolls around I can pick all the apples I want. Not just one time, but for as long as the tree produces apples—from one season to the next. And I never have to plant another apple tree. Why? Because of the seed I sowed in the ground years earlier. I've produced a perpetual supply.

Can you see how the two differ?

It's the difference in what I call having a "consumer mindset," and having a mindset of abundance. When I go to the market, I'm basically going there as a consumer. My goal usually is to buy things that will fill an immediate need—things that will be consumed in short order. I'm not thinking long-term, wondering if this will last me for a year or two, or three or four. I'm not thinking about planting, sowing or anything of the kind. I'm there as a consumer, and my sole purpose is making purchases for the now.

But when I plant a seed, my mindset is different. Now I'm thinking about the future. I'm believing that in due season the seed I've planted, the seed I've watered, nurtured and cultivated, is going to grow to produce an abundant crop or harvest. And, because I planted in good ground, good soil, I won't ever have to return during that season to replant. I won't just accumulate a one-time crop, but my harvest will come forth in abundance—over and over and over again!

There's an old expression that goes, *You reap what you sow*. Most often, this term is used as a form of chastisement—usually when someone is chided after they have done or said something wrong. The admonishment is that "everything you do has repercussions," or "you cannot escape the consequences of your actions." Even the Bible addresses it from a spiritual perspective in Galatians 6:7 where, in explaining the nature of God's justice, it says, "Be not deceived; God is not mocked: for whatsoever a man soweth, that shall he also reap." The *New Living Translation* says, "You will always harvest what you plant."

That's true with anything—whether it's the crops from your garden, the amount of grace you experience in relationships, or an increase in your finances—anything! Everything that exists does so because of a seed that was sown—planted, nurtured and cultivated—and grew to produce the corresponding harvest.

Seedtime and Harvest

Jesus gives us a clear picture of this in Mark 4, in a story He told His disciples that emphasized the principle of sowing and reaping. Jesus describes a farmer who went out to plant a crop in various ground conditions. In each instance, there were different results. Let's look in Matthew 4:3-8, *New International Version:*

> Listen! A farmer went out to sow his seed. As he was scattering the seed, some fell along the path, and the birds came and ate it up. Some fell on rocky places, where it did not have much soil. It sprang up quickly, because the soil was shallow. But when the sun came up, the plants were scorched, and they withered be-cause they had no root. Other seed fell among thorns, which grew up and choked the plants, so that they did not bear grain. Still other seed fell on good soil. It came up, grew and produced a crop, some multiplying thirty, some sixty, some a hundred times.

Let's examine the circumstances under which these seeds were sown. Some seeds fell "along the path," which means they never even touched the soil prepared to receive the seed. The seed remained exposed and became a quick meal for the birds that were flying overhead. Other seed fell "on rocky places," where there was little earth. Though the seed took root and began to grow, it didn't have strength to endure the elements because it wasn't planted deep enough to experience sufficient nourishment. The plants were quickly burned by the sun.

Still, other seeds landed "among thorns" and grew up, obviously giving the impression of an abundant crop. But it wasn't long before those plants were overtaken by the thorns which choked the life out of the plants.

Finally, there were seeds that fell "on good soil." And

because the soil was prepared to receive the seed, it took root, germinated and eventually blossomed—first into sprouts, then stems, and finally into an abundant harvest of fruit. The Bible said this crop increased as much as one hundredfold. Jesus used this analogy to show that when it comes to receiving the seed of His Word, people's hearts are represented by the ground type in each instance described. So, when we are endeavoring to live the life of abundance, we must properly position our hearts to become good ground for the "seed of abundance." If the Word is received only on the level of the intellect, it's exposed for the enemy to counter it with competing thoughts and ideas. If the Word is sown with only an emotional appreciation, then when challenges come we will not endure. If the Word is sown while remaining stressed over the cares of life, the Word will be choked and unable to release the life that's in it. So, the idea is to plant the seed of abundance deep in your heart and change your way of thinking, which will transform your way of life.

The Bible says the Word of God is your seed (Mark 4:14). Of all the biblical principles you will ever learn, the principles of sowing and reaping, seedtime and harvest, is perhaps the most important because nothing in the Kingdom can occur outside of seed. And how you handle your seed (the Word) will determine how you succeed and prosper in life.

The Farmer, the Seed, the Ground

In this parable in Mark 4, Jesus describes three essential elements that are necessary for a successful harvest to take place: the farmer, the seed, and the ground. For the sake of our study on the mindset of abundance, the farmer represents God; the seed represents His abundance, and the good ground is synonymous with the heart of the believer who will receive this Word by faith. If the believer will allow the seed of

God's Word to be sown in his heart, he can expect an abundant harvest of everything God's Word promises. That's what abundance, and living the abundant life, are all about. It's about taking in God's Word (the seed), believing and trusting it and Him, and allowing it to grow in your heart (the ground).

The Apostle Paul said it this way in 2 Corinthians 9:6, *New Living Translation*: "Remember this—a farmer who plants only a few seeds will get a small crop. But the one who plants generously will get a generous crop." What this conveys is that sowing always results in a harvest—whether it's small or large.

Sometimes, it's easier to show you how you may be working some of these principles, except that in many cases you are working them naturally. For example, why do you go to work each week? Some may go because they love their jobs, but most people go to work because they are hoping that at the end of the week they will receive a paycheck or some form of compensation. If you worked overtime, you're expecting your compensation to reflect your hours of labor.

It's a spiritual law that you will receive a harvest each time you sow (spiritual or material). Planting is equal to giving, and the Bible says we prosper from what we give. "Give, and [gifts] will be given to you; good measure, pressed down, shaken together, and running over, will they pour into [the pouch formed by] the bosom [of your robe and used as a bag]. For with the measure you deal out [with the measure you use when you confer benefits on others], it will be measured back to you" (Luke 6:38, *Amplified Bible, Classic Edition*). So, like the farmer, you have a right to expect a harvest on everything you give materially. Just make sure your motives are pure and right when you do give.

In the parable taught in Luke 8, Jesus makes it clear that the seed He is speaking of is the Word of God (verse 11). From that, we can understand that God's Word for us today is a prototype of all seed forms (including money). That's why it's important that we meditate the Word. Any attempt to walk in God's abundance without the seed of God's Word having first been planted or sown into your heart will, at its best, yield earthly treasure which is limited, vulnerable, and subject to destruction.

> Lay not up for yourselves treasures upon earth, where moth and rust doth corrupt, and where thieves break through and steal: But lay up for yourselves treasures in heaven, where neither moth nor rust doth corrupt, and where thieves do not break through nor steal: For where your treasure is, there will your heart be also. (Mark 6:19-21)

Abundance is not only a matter of the heart, but it is a mindset. By putting the Word in your heart and meditating on it, you position yourself to succeed in your thoughts concerning the Word you are planting—whether it's in your profession, health, family relationships, or your finances. It doesn't matter. It's God's principle of sowing and reaping, of seedtime and harvest at work on the inside of you. Good success, the kind that lasts, begins with the Word of God. But unless the seed of the Word is placed in good ground, until it gets off the pages of your Bible and is firmly planted in your heart, you will never experience the God-kind of success and abundance.

As a believer, you are considered a sower. God has given you His Word, and He expects you to use that Word to grow by. This happens by reading the Word, studying it, hiding or planting it in your heart so that it will spring forth and produce an abundance of itself in your life. It's just that simple. But it's not so simple if you're not using your seed properly—if you're not applying faith when you plant your seed. You must believe and receive that Word you speak into your life. When doing so, you are not considering the natural circumstances of your life and environment—only the Word which you are planting.

God: Your Seed Source

What about the source of your seed? Where does it come from?

Second Corinthians 9:10, in the *Amplified Bible, Classic Edition*, says, "And [God] Who provides seed for the sower."

It is God who is the Source of our seed. God gives seed to the sower. And what does He expect the sower to do with that seed? Plant it!

You see, God takes care of His own. He takes personal responsibility for providing seed for His children, expecting them to handle it the proper way. God takes personal responsibility for our abundance and increase in every area of our lives. That was part of His "provision plan" from the beginning, and it still holds true today.

From this you can see how having a poverty mindset and declaring such things over yourself as being broke, busted, and disgusted is a shameful indictment against your heavenly Father. He has taken personal care and responsibility to give you "richly all things to enjoy" (1 Timothy 6:17) in abundance by providing you seed to sow—increasing your fruit, so that not only do you have abundance, but you have enough to be a source of the Blessing to others.

Seek God's Kingdom First

We have discovered that the secret to experiencing God's abundance is the planting of His Word in our hearts. His Word is how we access the Kingdom and properly operate the rules of engagement for the Kingdom. This requires a mental reversal from the way in which we were taught to naturally think. Jesus frequently challenged natural thinking in His teachings and demonstrations of the Gospel.

When we pursue the kingdom of God, we become developed to the point that we can bypass things like worry, anxiety, and stress. Jesus literally taught us that as His kingdom becomes our reality, worry and anxiety over life's provision are eliminated. Why? Because God's abundant provision becomes our new reality. We are no longer conscious of lack and insufficiency. Matthew 6:31-33, *Amplified Bible, Classic Edition*, tells us,

> Therefore, do not worry and be anxious, saying, What are we going to have to eat? or, What are we going to have to drink? or, What are we going to have to wear? For the Gentiles (heathen) wish for *and* crave *and* diligently seek all these things, and your heavenly Father knows well that you need them all. But seek (aim at and strive after) first of all His kingdom and His righteousness (His way of doing and being right), and then all these things taken together will be given you besides.

One thing becomes very clear where abundance is concerned: You cannot be overly impressed with money, other-wise you will prohibit God's abundance from flourishing in your life. Your money and material wealth, and I mean all of it, must be at God's disposal to use as He wills. Only then can a man or woman experience the fullness of God's abundance in their life. I regularly say, "Tithing is elementary." The believer who will not tithe will struggle to enter in to God's abundance. It's not a matter of Old Covenant law, it's a matter of the condition of one's heart. The tithe keeps our heart conditioned toward God and His purposes. Jesus put it this way in Matthew 6:21, *New International Reader's Version:* "Your heart will be where your riches are." According to Malachi 3:10, the tithe produces such an abundance that "there shall not be room enough to receive it." A revelation of this will change your mind and change your life. This description is like that overflowing cup we talked about earlier—the one that can't help but spill over because it's so full that it can't hold any more. That's what it's like when God pours out so much on you that you can't take it all in. You don't have enough room to hold it all. Nor do you have enough lifetime to run out of it.

From this day forward, I want you to **Think Abundance!**

Your financial attitude and disposition should be in line with what God has said in His Word concerning money— from the tithe to the offering, obeying the Holy Spirit in giving, and adopting the lifestyle of giving. If your financial decisions are determined by the Word, you will see the outcome of harvest from those decisions. When you commit your finances to God, you'll never make decisions strictly based solely on money. When revelation of the Kingdom comes to you, the world's system will never guide your financial affairs.

When most people think abundance, they think money. They're convinced that money is the equivalent of prospering in God. But that's not what the Bible teaches. In fact, the Bible warns against becoming entangled with the enticement of money or anything material. Money itself is not good or bad. It's simply a tool. The danger lies in what Jesus referred to as the "spirit of mammon."

In summary, it's the spirit of greed that mismanages and perverts the use of money. First Timothy 6:10 says, "For the love of money is a root of all *kinds of* evil." Money, however, is a necessary tool used as a medium of exchange here on the earth. Abundance comes from an empowerment (called the Blessing) that causes an increase in one's life, including the increase of money. Proverbs 10:22, *Amplified Bible, Classic Edition*, says, "The blessing of the Lord—it makes [truly] rich, and He adds no sorrow with it [neither does toiling increase it]."

Money follows the Blessing—not the other way around!

Chapter Three

Abundance God's Way

Ask most people what they expect to be doing five, 10, 20 years from now, and chances are at least half of them will have an answer. They've already mapped out their lives and know (or at least they think they know) exactly where they're headed. If they're business-minded, most likely they will say they've planned a strategy they know will lead to a successful business venture. If their plan is to become a schoolteacher, doctor or lawyer, then they know they have a few more years of school ahead of them.

Whatever their plan, they're convinced it will lead to a successful career.

Actually, there's nothing wrong with that kind of thinking. After all, our nation is one regarded as the land of opportunity—a place where those who work hard, not making excuses but rather being dedicated and focused, can prosper. It's a resemblance of the Promised Land—a land of abundance that truly provides access to prosperity.

But what about the other half? What plans do they have for the future? Ask them, and they'll tell you they don't have a clue.

The truth is, none of us can fully predict where we will be or what we'll be doing a decade from now—especially if we are not yielded to God's plan for our lives. Most people aren't even confident enough in themselves to believe they can have a bright and prosperous future. Many haven't taken the time to consult God about His plan for their lives and what He has for them. They're so busy conforming to the world's way that God has been completely left out of the picture. If we consider only what seems right and reasonable, we could end up in a great deal of trouble. Proverbs 16:25, *New Living Translation*, says, "There is a path before each person that seems right, but it ends in *death*." In some translations, that word *death* is interpreted as *destruction*. In other words, you can get so caught up in doing things the way you think they should be done—mapping out your own strategies and planning how you want your life to go—that you miss God altogether. You can literally destroy your own life! This can cause you to never realize the abundance of God for you. But it doesn't have to be that way. Jeremiah 29:11-14, *New Living Translation*, says this about God's plans for you:

"For I know the plans I have for you," says the Lord. "They are plans for good and not for disaster, to give you a future and a hope. In those days when you pray, I will listen. If you look for me wholeheartedly, you will find me. I will be found by you," says the Lord.

I don't know how you interpret those verses, but to me it's a clear indication that God wants to be involved in our lives—that He *needs* to be involved if we're to prosper and succeed the way He has planned for us to. Read how *The Message* translates Jeremiah 29:11-13:

I know what I'm doing. I have it all planned out— plans to take care of you, not abandon you, plans to give you the future you hope for. When you call on me, when you come and pray to me, I'll listen. When you come looking for me, you'll find me.

God says He has your life "all planned out." And because He does, His plan will never change. Why? Because God doesn't change. He's always the same. He will never change His mind about you and what He wants to do for you. He knows what He's doing. He says in Isaiah 46:11, "Yea, I have spoken it, I will also bring it to pass; I have purposed it, I will also do it." Whatever God has purposed concerning your life cannot and will not be altered by the events that surround you. Unless, that is, you get in the middle of things with your own ideas and mess them up. That's what happened to Adam and Eve, as we've already seen.

His Way, Not Yours!

The Bible tells us clearly that our way of doing things is, in most cases, opposite of how God would do them or how He would instruct us to do them. Our orientation and training are of the natural order. Until our minds are renewed, we are less likely to think and act as God would in given situations and circumstances. When it comes to abundance, God has a prescribed way of doing and being right. As we meditate His Word, we come into alignment with the thoughts of God. It's difficult to hear from God with a carnal mind (a mind separated from divine influence).

God's kingdom is established and maintained by principles outlined in His Word, not principles established in the earth. Most abundance principles of the world are directly opposed to God's principles. The Kingdom of heaven is God's culture, values, morals, and laws of operation dispensed into the earth so that His abundance can be restored to the earth and to humanity. When you function according to Kingdom principles regarding the various areas of your life, you will experience God's abundance in those areas. Imagine God's culture and values being released in your business or your marriage. We pursue abundance God's way. He releases it through us as citizens of His kingdom. The Apostle Paul described us as "ambassadors." That means we have a diplomatic function in the earth to operate according to the rules of His kingdom (2 Corinthians 5:21).

Understand the Kingdom System

In understanding the Kingdom system, it's important to know that the kingdom of God is a "seed-based" system. Nothing happens in and through the Kingdom without the operations of seed. Look at Jesus' commentary on the kingdom of God in Mark 4:26-29:

> And He said, "The kingdom of God is as if a man should scatter seed on the ground, and should sleep by night and rise by day, and the seed should sprout and grow, he himself does not know how. For the earth yields crops by itself: first the blade, then the head, after that the full grain in the head. But when the grain ripens, immediately he puts in the sickle, because the harvest has come."

In these verses, Jesus describes the kingdom of God as a seed being planted. Notice the progression of the harvest, beginning with the planting of the seed: "First the blade, then the ear, after that the full corn in the ear." Just as seed is the foundation, the beginning of a plant's growth and development, the concept of the seed is the foundation for understanding the Kingdom.

In anything that involves increase or abundance, seed is always required. And, as we've already seen, the most valuable seed anyone could ever sow is the Word of God. Why? Because it takes the Word to sustain any level of increase in your life. There are people, for instance, who have lots of money. But because they don't have revelation, or spiritual understanding regarding the Kingdom's relationship to their money, their wealth is subject to loss. In the Kingdom, giving takes priority over buying and selling. Buying and selling is a worldly principle of abundance. Although there is nothing wrong with buying and selling, giving yields the greatest return in the kingdom of God.

Luke 6:38, *New Living Translation,* says "Give, and you will receive. Your gift will return to you in full—pressed down, shaken together to make room for more, running over, and poured into your lap." The principle of sowing and reaping comes from God. It's a heavenly, Kingdom principle that ensures a life of abundance here on earth.

A second concept is that God appoints a sower to every seed. The Bible says in 2 Corinthians 9:10, *Amplified Bible, Classic Edition:* "And [God] Who provides seed for the sower and bread for eating will also provide and multiply your [resources for] sowing and increase the fruits of your righteousness [which manifests itself in active goodness, kindness, and charity]." According to this verse, once planted, the seed has no choice but to grow and produce—to multiply. That's what seed does. It's also what the Word does. But notice how the seed manifests. The verse says it manifests itself in (1) bread for eating, and (2) more seed to sow, and (3) active goodness, kindness, and charity.

Anytime you sow or give materially to any cause that God leads you to give into, it will produce a threefold harvest. One third of the harvest is bread for you to eat. That's called *provision.* God has decided that, in your harvest, there must be provision. I find it interesting to see people trying to live off their jobs, their income, when God is trying to get them to live off their harvest. He said in your harvest is your provision. You can provide for yourself. His plan for your provision is, and always has been, through His principle of sowing and reaping. He intended for you to engage Kingdom principles so that you would always be provided for.

I am convinced that, while most people have resigned themselves to working a regular 9-to-5 job, that's not God's best for His people. I say that because I believe God doesn't want any of us tied down to a job, especially one that you don't like and enjoy. He wants you doing something every day that taps the potential that's on the inside of you, and not just to make a living and get by from day to day. Now, before you get overly excited; please understand I'm not saying you should quit your job. Not at all. But what I am saying is that you should be preparing to graduate from your job, to your work! What do I mean by that? Don't get to the place where you just settle for where you are, looking at how many years you have left before you can retire. Instead of being satisfied that you can retire in seven years, shrink that time. Say, "Lord, they say I can't retire for another seven years, but I know that's not the way we do things in the Kingdom. So, give me revelation as to how I can retire from this job one year from now so that I can get to my real work—my assignment; that thing that makes me want to get out of bed every day and attach myself to it."

The truth is, we do things because we think we must. And we think we must because we attach ourselves to the world's system. All the time, God is saying, *What about My kingdom? What about My way of doing things? You've never asked Me! What do you want to do? What do you enjoy doing? You were created to do that. You weren't created to run the grind until you retire, and then do it.*

A third concept is that every time seed is planted in the Kingdom, a harvest is produced. A single apple seed, for instance, will eventually produce an apple tree. And the harvest from that tree will be not one apple, but bushels of apples and potentially orchards. Similarly, sow into someone's life by blessing them, whether financially or otherwise, and you'll reap the harvest on that seed sown.

A fourth concept is this: Once harvest is reaped; a culture of generosity is established.

> Thus, you will be enriched in all things and in every way, so that you can be generous, and [your generosity-ty as it is] administered by us will bring forth thanks-giving to God. For the service that the ministering of this fund renders does not only fully supply what is lacking to the

saints (God's people), but it also overflows in many [cries of] thanksgiving to God (2 Corinthians 9:11-12, *Amplified Bible, Classic Edition)*.

Notice what's taking place in this scripture. There's an atmosphere of thanksgiving going on. Many cries of thanksgiving to God are being given, and by whom? God's people. But also, people who don't know God. People who are not born again. They're thanking God. Do you know why? Because God is blessing them through you. That's how God gets people's attention. He does things for them, things that quite often seem impossible in the natural. And He does them through His children—people like you and I. There will be times when God will tell you to do things, and He will specifically advise you to give.

Personally, He has instructed me to give and then tell the recipient, "God told me to give this to you and to let you know that He told me to do it. He wants you to know that it came from Him." In these cases, God knows their history with Him. He knows what needs to happen to get their attention, and He knows who to use. If that's you, then allow Him to use you to His glory so that others may be blessed.

This is a good place to invite you to make the following confession with me. Say these words aloud:

I receive the abundance of God. I live according to the Kingdom. I trust the kingdom of God in me. God's way of doing is the best plan for me, my life, and my finances. I am a giver! I sow into the Kingdom! I reap a mighty harvest. Inside of my harvest is abundance. Inside my harvest is everything I need for as long as I live, to do everything God has assigned me to do. I am blessed! I am fully supplied! I am wealthy! All my needs are met. I am out of debt! I have plenty more to put in store! In Jesus' Name. Amen!

Chapter Four

Why Think Abundance?

Because of the way God created us, and especially since we have come into Christ, our predisposition is abundance, not lack. Poverty is something we had to learn and be conditioned by to participate. The latter part of John 10:10 in the *New Living Translation* says, "My purpose is to give them a rich and satisfying life."

Notice those two words, *rich* and *satisfying*.

Obviously, one can be satisfied whether they have little or much. But being satisfied while having much is another matter altogether.

Look up the word *rich* in a dictionary, and some of the synonyms you'll find to describe what it means are words like: *prosperous, wealthy, well-off,* and *loaded.* Consideration of all these words taken together will bring you to one conclusion: *Abundance!*

Abundance, as we have already seen, is the process of planting seed into good soil, then nurturing it to maturity. It yields an abundant crop, or harvest. For many people, the perspective they have of abundance is wrong and must change. Abundance is not limited to money and material goods, although it doesn't exclude them either. Therefore, abundance is not about hoarding and accumulating material wealth unto ourselves. God has an agenda for abundance that includes the demonstration of the Gospel message to the world.

We see that hoarding mentality in a story Jesus tells in Luke 12 about a man who was well-off:

> And he spake a parable unto them, saying, The ground of a certain rich man brought forth plentifully: And he

thought within himself, saying, What shall I do, because I have no room where to bestow my fruits? And he said, This will I do: I will pull down my barns and build greater; and there will I bestow all my fruits and my goods (verses 16-18).

Although this man had much, he did not *think* abundance. His mind was preoccupied with accumulation. Here's where the problem came in: When the harvest came in, he realized how much he had. I like to say, "he started counting." If you're more conscious of counting than you are receiving, it's likely that you have not arrived into God's abundance yet. This man never switched in his thinking from "being blessed" to "being a blessing." Instead, he came up with a plan to stockpile and showcase his achievements when it is clear God wanted to use him as a force of good and favor to cities and nations in his region.

Verse 18 says the man looked at his abundant harvest and said, "This will I do: I will pull down my barns and build greater; and there will I bestow all my fruits and my goods." There is nothing wrong with building bigger barns or bigger warehouses in which to store your abundant supply. Abundant harvest requires a larger capacity. Anytime you are dealing in abundance, there is always a consideration as to how to manage it most efficiently. But the other side of abundance is distribution; it creates an atmosphere for giving. It empowers you to release the good of God to others. It distinguishes you from the rest because the act of true generosity is rarely seen by the world through the Church.

And I will make of you a great nation, and I will bless you [with abundant increase of favors] and make your name famous and distinguished, and you will be a blessing [dispensing good to others]. — **Genesis 12:2**, *Amplified Bible, Classic Edition*

When you *think* abundance, it becomes easy to receive and to give. The quantity of your giving is never regulated by logic and natural financial rules. A man or woman who thinks abundance never concedes to "running out." The abundance of God, once revealed, is inexhaustible, limitless, and boundless.

To me, though I am the very least of all the saints (God's consecrated people), this grace (favor, privilege) was granted and graciously entrusted: to proclaim to the Gentiles the unending (boundless, fathomless, incalculable, and exhaustless) riches of Christ [wealth which no human being could have searched out].
—Ephesians 3:8

Managing Your Thoughts About Abundance

How you think will determine which force you will attract—abundance or lack. Everyone has some degree of supply, whether very little or very much or something in between. Your thoughts regarding your specific level of supply, or supply in general, will determine how you manage increase once you experience it. When you engage in the world's system of financial law, everything you have is subject to complete and absolute loss. Kingdom rules of financial engagement come with protection, preservation, and a growth plan. Jesus warned us to not put our confidence in earthly treasures. This doesn't mean we don't deal financially with the world. It means we don't trust the world's systems to prosper us to the degree that we see them as our source. Matthew 6:19-21 warns us against doing so:

> Lay not up for yourselves treasures upon earth, where moth and rust doth corrupt, and where thieves break through and steal: But lay up for yourselves treasures in heaven, where neither moth nor rust doth corrupt, and where thieves do not break through nor steal: For

where your treasure is, there will your heart be also.

We must allow God, through His Word, to change our mindset regarding money and increase. Otherwise, our hearts (motivations, purposes, and intents) will be misdirected and misguided by placing value on the wrong things. Without His Word influencing our thoughts, we will find ourselves trying to serve the spirit of mammon (greed) and God at the same time. This is impossible. One will inevitably win over the other because our heart was never created to be divided. Matthew 6:24, *New International Version*, says, "No one can serve two masters. Either you will hate the one and love the other, or you will be devoted to the one and despise the other. You cannot serve both God and money."

Increase is on God's mind. It should be on your mind as well. Keep your thoughts in the arena of abundance, regardless of the circumstances or situations you currently face. The circumstances or situations must change as you realign your thoughts with the thoughts of God.

Psalm 115:14 says, "The Lord shall increase you more and more, you and your children." We could spend hours researching words like *increase, excess, more,* and *overflow*. But it all comes down to one simple truth: God desires to give His children a lifestyle of abundance. When you trust Him as your Source, abundance will flow. The psalmist David put it this way in Psalm 23:1: "The Lord is my shepherd; I shall not want." As we acknowledge God as our Shepherd (Guide, Protector, Defender, Provider), we will not experience lack of anything we need to complete our assignment. He has guaranteed care over our lives and strategy for bringing His abundance into our hands.

Wealth is a tool God uses to facilitate abundance to you, and through you to others. Your attitude must be right regarding abundance for it to be attracted to you and properly flow through you. God admonishes you to stay mindful that He is the responsible party for true riches in your life. But He empowers you with all the tools you need to cause wealth, or abundant harvest, to flow toward you.

Chapter Five

The Practicality of Abundance Thinking

There are at least three factors that contribute to living in God's abundance.

The first is knowledge. It's impossible to think on a level where there is no knowledge for that level of thinking. Second is wisdom and discretion. God's gifts and provision are first spiritual, not natural. So, to receive His abundance requires that your thought processes be in alignment with His wisdom so that you can discern how to apply the knowledge.

Thirdly, there's the faith factor. Because abundance comes from the spiritual realm, faith is a must if you're going to access that realm. Logic and reasoning will never get you there.

Abundance thinking comes when you bring all three of these factors together, which is what we find in Joshua 1:8: "Study this Book of Instruction continually. Meditate on it day and night so you will be sure to obey everything written in it. Only then will you prosper and succeed in all you do" (*New Living Translation*). Spending time rehearsing God's thoughts about abundance through His Word positions you to hear clearly from Him and to know what and how to think in any given situation. As you take your eyes off the world and its problems, and begin to focus on God and His Word, you will be encouraged and inspired to step out in faith, trusting Him to give you clear direction. This is what sets you apart from those who are acting on knowledge alone, without the benefit of Godly wisdom that produces revelation. Practical measures alone will yield limited and natural results. Practical measures for the believer are vain and useless unless discerned by the wisdom of God and applied by faith in His Word.

Necessary Knowledge

It's interesting to see how most people think and live when it comes to experiencing abundance. Most never consider that God just might have something better for them, or more for them. If their circumstances cause them to prosper financially, then fine. If not, then they resign themselves to thoughts like: *Maybe God did not intend for everyone to prosper.* Or, *I guess I'm just doomed to a life of poverty and lack.* They reason themselves into believing that it's not God's will for them to have abundance. What I have learned is that abundance will come to those who think it and believe it—especially, and in a distinct fashion for God's children.

Thinking defeat, failure, and poverty is exactly what the Lord speaks to in Hosea 4:6, where He declares: "My people are destroyed for lack of knowledge." The *New Living Translation* says, "My people are being destroyed because they don't know me." *The Message* says, "My people are ruined because they don't know what's right or true." In each of these translations, it's clear that people are perishing: their lives are being destroyed because of ignorance—of God and His Word.

Remember the farmer we discussed in an earlier chapter? The farmer must have a certain level of knowledge to plant seed properly as a basis for expecting a good crop. He's not just some novice who tosses seed into the ground without regard for the season, the ground, and the means of irrigation for that seed. He plants with knowledge. There are practical levels of knowledge needed to engage spiritual laws. Regardless of how much faith you profess to have, you cannot simply go out into the field and expect corn to come up where you have no knowledge that corn seed has been planted. There is nothing automatic in the Kingdom. It's a seed-based system and you must develop your knowledge of sowing and reaping to function in it. Even the study of natural seed and the germination process can lend great insight into the spiritual process of planting the Word into your heart.

The enemy perpetuates the spirit of poverty to bring shame, disgrace and embarrassment, and reproach on the Body of Christ. When the believer lives cut off from access to the Father's abundance, it makes for a bad reflection on his heavenly Father. Knowledge of truth regarding this area sheds light in the mind and heart of the believer to establish new expectations and standards for living.

The unfolding of your words gives light; it gives understanding to the simple. **—Psalm 119:130,** *New International Version*

This is the power of the Word. It stops ignorance in its tracks. It dispels darkness and sheds light on God's intents and purposes for us; regardless of religious orientation, family tradition, or customs. When the revelation of the Father and His kingdom is unveiled within you, everything changes!

Get Godly Wisdom

We look around and wonder why so many Christians today are struggling, living paycheck to paycheck and never seeming to get ahead in life. The answer is simple: If I know more, I can have more. Whatever is revealed to me can then be restored to me. Knowledge of truth is one thing. However, application of that truth makes all the difference in your life. Many believers *agree* with God's Word, but don't *believe* God's Word. The difference is found in the application of His Word. Action proves believing. You must have God's wisdom to properly apply His principles of abundance.

Godly wisdom is easy to acquire. James 1:5, *New International Version,* says, "If any of you lacks wisdom, you should ask God, who gives generously to all without finding fault, and it will be given to you."

You can either do one or the other. You can complain that you don't have what you need and therefore don't know what to do. Or, you can follow these practical instructions found in James 1:5 and enter into God's abundance.

Without Godly wisdom for abundance-thinking and living, you will look to the world's system for answers to your problems. God's way will be an after-thought. These are those who say the same things and use the same methods the world uses to get ahead. And just like everyone else who puts their trust in man instead of God, they're finding out that it doesn't work. They're learning that the tricks and trades of man are nothing more than temporary solutions. They may work for a while, but they don't last. People who think this way usually try to get God to bless something they have devised. Why do that when you have direct access to divine strategies that are already blessed?

In Proverbs 4:7-9, *The Message*, the Bible pairs wisdom with knowledge, or understanding. It says, "Above all and before all, do this: Get Wisdom! Write this at the top of your list: Get Understanding! Throw your arms around her - believe me, you won't regret it; never let her go - she'll make your life glorious. She'll garland your life with grace, she'll festoon your days with beauty."

From this passage it's easy to see how applying God's wisdom to any circumstance can ensure good results. That goes hand in hand with the instructions of Matthew 6:33 to seek God and His righteousness first so that "all these things shall be added to you." What *things* is the verse referring to? All the things you need to live an abundant, healthy, successful, and joyful life. Understanding God and His Word, and exercising His wisdom in the decisions you make, will always lead you to compliance with His will and purposes for your life.

So, how does faith work with these two elements of understanding and applying wisdom? James 2:14-16 asks, "What *does it* profit, my brethren, if someone says he has faith but does not have works? Can faith save him? If a brother or sister is naked and destitute of daily food, and one of you says to them, 'Depart in peace, be warmed and filled,' but you do not give them the things which are needed for the body, what *does* it profit?"

We find the answers in verses 17: "Thus also faith by itself, if it does not have works (practical applications and proofs), is dead...." (my emphasis)

Faith and works are necessary companions for true abundance to manifest. When you have faith, it will produce works that have been accomplished by the process of combining natural knowledge with spiritual wisdom. Works don't produce faith, but faith produces the works of God. *Works* are "actions of obedience that result from faith with the application or discernment through knowledge."

Chapter Six

Abundance Is a Revelation

Did you know that supply was already in existence before there was ever a need? That's evidenced by what the Scripture says in the first chapter of Genesis, the very first book of the Bible, which gives us a chronology of Creation and how God formed and fashioned both Heaven and Earth. We won't examine the entire process here, but if you'll take time to read it for yourself, you'll find that not only is God the Master of creativity, He is extremely orderly in how He creates—from the creation of the heavens and earth to the fowl of the air and the fish of the sea, from the plants and animals and ultimately to mankind.

For now, let's look at verses 9-12 in that first chapter to see how the earth came into being.

> And God said, Let the waters under the heavens be collected into one place [of standing], and let the dry land appear. And it was so. God called the dry land Earth, and the accumulated waters He called Seas. And God saw that this was good (fitting, admirable) *and* He approved it. And God said, Let the earth put forth [tender] vegetation: plants yielding seed and fruit trees yielding fruit whose seed is in itself, each according to its kind, upon the earth. And it was so. The earth brought forth vegetation: plants yielding seed according to their own kinds and trees bearing fruit in which was their seed, each according to its kind. And God saw that it was good (suitable, admirable) *and* He approved it. (*Amplified Bible, Classic Edition*)

Now read and see how God carved out a special place for mankind on the Earth—a garden He called Eden.

> The Lord God planted a garden eastward in Eden, and there He put the man whom He had formed. And out of the ground the Lord God made every tree grow that is pleasant to the sight and good for food. The tree of life *was* also in the midst of the garden, and the tree of the knowledge of good and evil. (Genesis 2:8-9).

Notice the progression that took place: First, God created the Earth. Next, He "formed man from the dust of the ground and breathed into his nostrils the breath or spirit of life, and man became a living being" (Genesis 2:7, *Amplified Bible, Classic Edition*). Then, He made provision. He created a garden filled with "every tree that is pleasant to the sight or to be desired— good (suitable, pleasant) for food." And finally: "…there he placed the man he had made. The Lord God made all sorts of trees grow up from the ground—trees that were beautiful and that produced delicious fruit" (Genesis 2:8-9, *New Living Translation*).

An abundance of *provision* is one of the top pursuits of mankind today. The good news is that through Jesus, God has provided for us in every way possible, so that we never have need for anything as long as we live on the earth. Starting with Adam, He gave us fellowship with Himself, a life assignment, and every provision to meet the need of fulfilling our assignment here on earth. Adam, through his disobedience, caused a disruption in the flow of God's intent toward humanity. But Jesus (the last Adam) came to restore all that Adam lost and to reposition us back into fellowship with the Father. He came to re-establish our assignment and make abundant provision for everything we need to fulfill the assignment on our life. For us, it's called living in the kingdom of God (our "new" Garden).

When we yielded to the lordship of Jesus, we entered the kingdom of God. We entered a total life of provision, purpose, and fellowship. Because of these provisions, we must live and act as though we have them in full so that we can reach our destiny. It begins by developing a new mindset. We must shift our thinking so that it lines up with what God has spoken in His Word, and not according to our natural circumstances. Most Christians live life as it is shaped by their natural circumstances and conditions. They think they have no option or choice in the matter. This is not true. When you spend time meditating what God has said regarding life, you receive a revelation and His Words become your strongest reality. This results in a transformation of your thinking which directly transforms your life. The Apostle Paul refers to it in Romans 12:2 as "renewing" the mind. He said, "And do not be conformed to this world, but be transformed by the renewing of your mind, that you may prove what is that good and acceptable and perfect will of God."

In other words, when we embrace transformation through renewing our thinking based on God's Word, we are empowered to reject conformity to the world's way of living and demonstrate God's original intent for humanity. We live a life that becomes a picture of God's will, which is good, acceptable, and perfect in every way.

Now I understand more clearly Jesus' teaching in Matthew 6 regarding the importance of having the proper perspective on provision in life:

> Therefore I tell you, stop being [a]perpetually uneasy (anxious and worried) about your life, what you shall eat *or what you shall drink*; or about your body, what you shall put on. Is not life greater [in quality] than food, and the body [far above and more excellent] than clothing? ... But seek ([a]aim at and strive after) first of all His kingdom and His righteousness ([b] His way of doing and being right), and then all these things [c]taken together will be given you besides (verses 25, 33, *Amplified Bible Classic Edition*).

Living a life of God's abundance is not as simple as reading this book, or the Bible for that matter. Neither is it a matter of occasional prayer or statements of confession spoken only in times of need. Once God's abundance is revealed to you, it becomes real to you. To live and walk in God's abundance requires at least three things: knowledge of the truth, faith to embrace the truth, and wisdom to apply the truth. This combination yields revelation of God's plans and purposes for you and yields success and prosperity in life— the abundant life.

The Power of Revelation

From Psalm 119:130 we learn that the source of revelation is found in the unfolding of the Word of God to our spirit-man. It says, "The entrance of Your words gives light; it gives understanding to the simple."

Then we learn in 1 Corinthians 2:9-10 that the giver and distributor of that revelation is the Holy Spirit:

> But as it is written: "Eye has not seen, nor ear heard, Nor have entered into the heart of man The things which God has prepared for those who love Him." But God has revealed *them* to us through His Spirit. For the Spirit searches all things, yes, the deep things of God.

Jesus said, the Holy Spirit has been sent to teach us all things and to bring all things to our remembrance (John 14:26). So, it is my assessment that you were never intended to go and do what you first cannot see. Revelation produces spiritual insight that dictates what you see naturally. It's inner vision that enhances your outer, or natural vision (perspective), so you are aware and enlightened—never deceived— and empowered to maneuver in your assignment and toward your destiny with speed and accuracy. With revelation, you will never see lack and insufficiency

—only abundance! Through the Holy Spirit God, is unfolding His plan of abundance that meets every need in your life.

The Bible gives us a good picture of how revelation works in 2 Kings 6:15-17:

> And when the servant of the man of God arose early and went out, there was an army, surrounding the city with horses and chariots. And his servant said to him, "Alas, my master! What shall we do?" So he answered, "Do not fear, for those who are with us *are* more than those who *are* with them." And Elisha prayed, and said, "Lord, I pray, open his eyes that he may see." Then the Lord opened the eyes of the young man, and he saw. And behold, the mountain was full of horses and chariots of fire all around Elisha.

This passage provides evidence that revelation determines what you see—and how you respond to natural conditions around you. When you read the entire context of this event in 2 Kings you will find that the servant had every natural reason to be intimidated and afraid of what he saw with his natural eyes. His problem, however, was that he could not see spiritually until the prophet prayed that his eyes be opened. This tells me that you can pray for revelation for yourself and others. When he went back to "look" again he saw with the eyes of his spirit-man and perceived the abundance of provision for his protection and care.

The other aspect of revelation is that it produces "rest" for those who can see it. Notice, the prophet never went outside to see for himself the conditions the servant feared. He was able to see by the Spirit, which allowed him to rest, but the servant was fretful. While the servant only had "information" or facts to go on, the prophet was operating at the superior level of "revelation." **Before you can *have***

abundance, you must first be able to *see* your abundance. It's not that the prophet was not aware of the clear and present danger, he simply possessed a greater consciousness of the abundance of provision and protection.

Revelation changes your thinking, which changes your life. It changes the way you respond to the enemy, and negative circumstances that are designed to motivate you to fear. There was a major difference in the behavior of the prophet and servant. While revelation caused one to trust, information caused the other to fear.

From this day forward, I believe you will never fear lack or not having enough to complete your assignment. You will live out of a revelation of God's abundance for your life and you will manifest everything you need in life.

Many people, including Christians, give greater significance to education than they do to revelation. The reason this is so is because they have not experienced the benefit of revelation in their lives. For most, education is their only ticket to achieving success and becoming someone. But the truth is, regardless of how important education is, it's not going to give you the advantages that spiritual revelation provides. Revelation is advanced knowledge that cannot be learned in a formal setting. It is discerned by the spirit of man from the Spirit of God.

In Joshua 1:8, the Lord spoke words to the prophet and said: "This Book of the Law shall not depart from your mouth, but you shall meditate in it day and night, that you may observe to do according to all that is written in it. For then you will make your way prosperous, and then you will have good success." The *New Living Translation* says, "Study this Book of Instruction continually. Meditate on it day and night so you will be sure to obey everything written in it. Only then will you prosper and succeed in all you do."

So, you see, the meditation of God's Word is what results in revelation. Reading alone does not produce light, nor does it produce understanding. You must plant the Word of God in your heart and mind, making it part of your consciousness. Then, and only then, will it take root and begin to work for you.

If you're a believer, then you have capacity to see beyond your current circumstances. You have the same faith as God. You are created in His image and you share in His divine nature.

> Grace and peace be multiplied to you in the knowledge of God and of Jesus our Lord, as His divine power has given to us all things that *pertain* to life and godliness, through the knowledge of Him who called us by glory and virtue, by which have been given to us exceedingly great and precious promises, that through these you may be partakers of the divine nature, having escaped the corruption *that is* in the world through lust. — 2 Peter 1:2-4

In Ephesians 1:17-19, *Amplified Bible, Classic Edition*, the Apostle Paul writes: "[For I always pray to] the God of our Lord Jesus Christ, the Father of glory, that He may grant you a spirit of wisdom and revelation [of insight into mysteries and secrets] in the [deep and intimate] knowledge of Him, by having the eyes of your heart flooded with light, so that you can know and understand the hope to which He has called you, and how rich is His glorious inheritance in the saints (His set-apart ones)."

Just like Paul prayed for the church at Ephesus, you can pray for others and for yourself. You can receive the granting of revelation in your life. You can ask God to open the eyes of your heart, so that they might be flooded with the light of His Word and bring the kind of spiritual revelation that enables you to know the richness of your inheritance in Him.

Once you are in Christ and Christ is in you, revelation is your inheritance. However, it must be believed, received and acted upon. The revelation you need is already in you. God has already given it to you. As your mind is renewed to the revelation of abundance, your spirit is transformed to accept nothing less.

Revelation Yields Unlimited Possibilities

One other advantage we find attached to revelation is that it yields unlimited possibilities that ultimately lead to abundance. The story of Abram and his nephew, Lot, is a good example of what I'm talking about. God instructed Abram to pack up and leave Egypt, taking only his immediate family with him:

> Now the Lord had said to Abram: "Get out of your country, from your family and from your father's house, to a land that I will show you. I will make you a great nation; I will bless you and make your name great; and you shall be a blessing. I will bless those who bless you, and I will curse him who curses you; and in you all the families of the earth shall be bless-ed." (Genesis 12:1-3)

But in Genesis 13:5-7, we find that an extended family member also took the journey with Abram. Lot, Abram's nephew, had tremendously increased because of his association with Abram. However, we also see that Abram paid a price for this slight deviation from the instructions God gave him regarding not bringing kindred along with him.

> Lot also, who went with Abram, had flocks and herds and tents. Now the land was not able to support them, that they might dwell together, for their possessions were so great that they could not dwell together. And

there was strife between the herdsmen of Abram's livestock and the herdsmen of Lot's livestock. The Canaanites and the Perizzites then dwelt in the land.

Once Abram received revelation and negotiated Lot's separation (verses 8-13), there was a realignment into the will and purpose of God for Abram's life. He saw increase and a new level of unlimited abundance.

> And the Lord said to Abram, after Lot had separated from him: "Lift your eyes now and look from the place where you are—northward, southward, east-ward, and westward; for all the land which you see I give to you and your descendants forever. And I will make your descendants as the dust of the earth; so that if a man could number the dust of the earth, *then* your descendants also could be numbered. Arise, walk in the land through its length and its width, for I give it to you.

Notice how God has now released Abram to "look and see" in every possible direction for his advancement and abundant increase. There were no more restraints in the possibilities for Abram's future.

The Message, verses 14-17, says, "Open your eyes, look around. Look north, south, east, and west. Everything you see, the whole land spread out before you, I will give to you and your children forever. I'll make your descendants like dust—counting your descendants will be as impossible as counting the dust of the Earth. So—on your feet, get moving! Walk through the country, its length and breadth; I'm giving it all to you."

It is interesting to note that both Abram and Lot were walking in a level of abundance before the separation, but what Abram experienced after Lot's departure was mind-blowing. There are some things that cannot be revealed to you as long as you keep a "Lot" in your life. Abundance was destined for Abram's life. But strict obedience to the Father's instruction for your life will guarantee God's best in His abundance for you.

If you're waiting for God's abundance to show up in your life, and wondering why nothing's happening, ask yourself: Are there any "Lots" in my life; any distractions that are holding me back from the revelation of God's purpose and receiving His abundance? When God reveals those distractions to you, whatever they are, be quick to move them out of the way. This will open the door for His abundance to begin to flow.

Chapter Seven

Abundance is a Mindset

The life of God's abundance requires a change of mind. More important than *what* you think is *how* you're thinking.

The Bible says in Romans 12:2, *New King James Version*, "And do not be conformed to this world, but be transformed by the renewing of your mind, that you may prove what is that good and acceptable and perfect will of God." Read how that verse is translated in *The Message*. But let's begin with the first verse so you get the entire picture.

> So here's what I want you to do, God helping you: Take your everyday, ordinary life—your sleeping, eating, going-to-work, and walking-around life—and place it before God as an offering. Embracing what God does for you is the best thing you can do for him. Don't become so well-adjusted to your culture that you fit into it without even thinking. Instead, fix your attention on God. You'll be changed from the inside out. Readily recognize what he wants from you, and quickly respond to it. Unlike the culture around you, always dragging you down to its level of immaturity, God brings the best out of you, develops well-formed maturity in you.

Can you see what Paul is saying here? He's saying you can no longer live the way you used to—conformed to the current culture and subscribing to the existing standards of society. He says, "You're no longer ordinary and you cannot afford to live like you are. Instead, you are to embrace what God has done for you and *fix your attention* on that. When you do, you'll be changed from the inside out."

Your mind is one of the things God's Word will change. Why? This is the only way God can facilitate His abundance through you. His Word expands your capacity to embrace the big ideas and plans He desires to facilitate through you to humanity.

Again, the word *abundance* means "an extremely plentiful and an over sufficient quantity of supply." In layman terms, it simply means "rich."

Throughout the Bible we find example after example that demonstrates God's attitude toward His people and His will that they live prosperously and in His abundant supply. One of the most notable scriptures is 3 John 2, which says: "Beloved, I pray that you may prosper in every way and [that your body] may keep well, even as [I know] your soul keeps well *and* prospers" *(Amplified Bible, Classic Edition)*. That same theme resonates through Matthew 6:25.

> Therefore I tell you, stop being perpetually uneasy (anxious and worried) about your life, what you shall eat *or what you shall drink;* or about your body, what you shall put on.

Just as in the case of abundance, worrying is also a mindset. In the same fashion in which it takes a conscious effort to think abundance, the same is true regarding worry. I call the mindset of worry "biblical meditation in reverse." If you can worry, then you also can meditate God's Word and eliminate worry from your mind and life. By changing the focus of your thoughts and replacing it with the Word of God, stress, anxiety, and worry regarding supply and abundance in life will go away altogether.

Living In God's Reality

Jesus said in Matthew 6:33: "But seek first the kingdom of God and His righteousness, and all these things shall be added to you." *The Message* says, "Steep your life in God-reality, God-initiative, God-provisions. Don't worry about missing out. You'll find all your everyday human concerns will be met."

Worry is not a God-reality. It's a natural response to a natural reality. It's how the world trains you to think. You hear people saying things like, "I'm just so worried." That's a natural response to a natural reality. Or, they might say, "My business is in trouble. I'm worried that I may have to file bankruptcy." Again, these words represent a natural response (worry and anxiety) to a worldly or natural reality! These words represent a mental attitude that is entirely contradictory to the purpose and plan of God for you and your situations.

There is no worry in God's reality. God-reality is a state of mind where there is no stress, no fret, no anxiety. It took me a while to learn that important truth, but once I did, it became my way of life. And I'm sure glad about it. Because of it, I've learned to absorb the peace of God. The interesting thing is that I didn't become stress-free by dumping stress. I became stress-free by loading up on God's peace. I took God's Word concerning His peace, and I began to meditate on it. It changed my thoughts. Instead of worrying about certain things, I began to meditate on what God's Word had to say about those things. I renewed my mind to the things of God, and not the things which I had previously worried about. As a result, stress was escorted out of my life and peace was escorted into my life. You can do the same thing. You can steep your life in God-reality, and before you know it worry will be a thing of the past.

The primary means by which worry and stress are removed from your life is through revelation. That's because revelation produces a mindset that is consistent with a new spiritual reality—it's that God-reality which I keep referring to. I like to say that the mind is like a thermostat that creates or controls the temperature of your life. Whatever temperature you want to be in your life will be determined by the set-ting of your thermostat. The thing is, God is not going to do it for you. He gives you the ability to set your own thermostat.

Your mind is designed to give you imagery through your imagination. How you use your imagination will determine your boundaries and placement of limitations.

The story of the Tower of Babel is a good example of this. In it, we see where a group of ungodly people decided to build a city and a tower designed to reach into the heavens. The Bible says that God came down to see the construction project, and quickly put an end to this effort. We learn so much from the commentary God made regarding this project:

Genesis 11:6 says, "And the Lord said, Behold, they are one people and they have all one language; and this is only the beginning of what they will do, and now nothing they have imagined they can do will be impossible for them" *(Amplified Bible, Classic Edition).*

This is a powerful revelation. Here is how this passage speaks to me. Money, people, and natural resources do not create the standard of limitation regarding what I can do. God cites here that if I can imagine it based on speaking in harmony with what I believe, whatever I imagine shall come to pass!

Another important note is that there is no Godly endorsement for accomplishing something that is contrary to His purposes and plans for your life.

God stopped this work from being completed (verses 7-9). Why? Because it was not a work of God. It was purely a work of the flesh or a natural plan without regard for God's intent or purpose. This is a major problem with many Christians today. They come up with an idea that perhaps is noble and convince themselves that it's something God wants them to do. The problem is, they never consulted with God, nor did they have His backing. They made a decision that did not include Him. Proverbs 14:12 says, "There is a way that seems right to a man, but its end is the way of death."

Replace Negative Words With Truth

Instead of speaking negative things, replace them with words that line up with the Word of God. When poverty raises its ugly head, or when lack tries to invade your space, you must have one response and one response only. Say, "It is written that My God supplies everything I need according to His riches in glory by Christ Jesus" (Philippians 4:19). When sickness tries to attack your body and rob you of the abundance of health and peace, when shame, fear, guilt, and condemnation try to steal from you the righteousness of God in Christ, take claim to what God has provided for you through Jesus and defy the authority of those elements of the curse. Refuse to allow those forces to operate with authority in your life. Say, "I've been redeemed from the curse (the authority of sin, sickness, disease, poverty and lack). I receive the Blessing that has been bestowed upon me through Jesus Christ (Galatians 3:13-14).

Some take issue with confessions such as this because, for them, they think they are unreasonable and impossible to materialize. But the truth is, words like these lines up perfectly with God and His Word. They are spirit and they represent the truest reality of what God has planned and purposed for His children. I will not stop confessing and believing until God's reality become my reality.

Living a prosperous life, and having the things we need and more, is part of our inheritance as God's children. It's also what Jesus intended when He came to the earth (John 10:10). The point to remember is that true abundance (spiritual and material) comes from God and is intended to occur without toil. Toil is highly unnecessary! To toil is to exert more physical and mental effort than is necessary to reach one's desired outcomes. The reason I say that toil [struggling, striving, and surviving] is unnecessary is because we have been endowed with the Blessing. Proverbs 10:22 says this about the Blessing: "The blessing of the Lord makes one rich, and He adds no sorrow with it." The *Amplified Bible, Classic Edition,* says, "The blessing of the Lord—it makes [truly] rich, and He adds no sorrow with it **[neither does toiling increase it]."**

Your faith in the Blessing is truly all you need. Prepare to receive God's Blessing into your life. Receive it now! The sooner you believe it and receive it, the Blessing will manifest and work for you.

Embracing the Truth

It is imperative that as you read this book, you position your heart and mind to embrace truth as opposed to the natural reality of your current experience. The Word of God (the teachings of Jesus), is the highest truth. Never allow negative or adverse circumstance to establish your reality. Permit your reality to come from God's intended purpose and plans. Jesus said in John 8:32, *New Living Translation,* "You will know the truth, and the truth will set you free." Truth eliminates all bondage and deception rendered by wrong thoughts, ideas and philosophies.

Whatever systems of thought you possess that produce distortion in your life can be removed and eradicated by truth. Each of us was born into the world with ungodly thought patterns. If you're ever going to live the life of abundance God has planned and purposed for you, then you must settle in your mind that abundance is truth, and lack is a lie; that not having enough is of the enemy but having more than enough is of God. If you don't take hold of this truth, the enemy will use his lies to confine you with the deception of lack, insufficiency, and abject poverty.

Rational thinking and logic are always inferior to truth. Truth is never confined to or validated by the processes of logic and rationale. First Corinthians 2:14, *New Living Translation,* says, "But people who aren't spiritual can't receive these truths from God's Spirit. It all sounds foolish to them and they can't understand it, for only those who are spiritual can understand what the Spirit means." The natural mind must become a student of the Holy Spirit. Without the mind of the Spirit, your natural mind will misinterpret truth every time you hear it. Romans 8:6-7, *Amplified Bible, Classic Edition,* says: "Now the mind of the flesh [which is sense and reason without the Holy Spirit] is death [death that comprises all the miseries arising from sin, both here and hereafter]. But the mind of the [Holy] Spirit is life and [soul] peace [both now and forever]. [That is] because the mind of the flesh [with its carnal thoughts and purposes] is hostile to God, for it does not submit itself to God's Law; indeed it cannot."

Your surrender to the mind of Christ will keep you thinking and functioning at the level of God. It will keep you above and beyond the limitation of normal and natural living. You were created to live supernaturally so that you may perform at the place that allows for the manifestation of "greater works" (John 14:12) in and through you.

Chapter Eight

The Place of Abundance

There is a "place of abundance." As you now have a good idea of God's attitude toward abundance for His children, and what it means to have faith for abundance, how do we now position ourselves to receive abundance? This is what I refer to as being in the "place of abundance." It is inclusive of your spiritual posture and mental positioning in receiving this revelation.

Many people are seeking God's abundance, but they are looking for it by the wrong means and in the wrong places. Let me show you what I mean by first offering a clear definition of spiritual abundance.

As we have already determined, the dictionary defines *abundance* with terms like: "an extremely plentiful or over sufficient quantity or supply," "overflowing fullness," "affluence" and "wealth." But looking at two passages of scripture, we get a more complete and advanced definition.

First, in Ephesians 3:20 the Word refers to God's ability. It is described as "exceeding, abundantly, and above" all that you are able to think, articulate, or imagine. However, there is only one way in which God's ability can be experienced by the believer. This happens when the believer "works His Word [power] within them." The significance of this passage of scripture is that you and I will never be able to think, articulate, imagine, hope, or dream beyond God's ability to perform. But on the other hand, God's ability to perform through you is limited to your capacity to think, articulate, imagine, hope and dream. God's abundance is immeasurable and cannot be contained within the confines of economy. Therefore, the place of abundance is found in the meditation of the Word or the "working of the Word (or His power) within me." The more of His power or His Word I yield to, the more of His abundance I experience.

The next description of abundance is found in 2 Corinthians 9:8, *Amplified Bible, Classic Edition*: "

> And God is able to make all grace (every favor and earthly blessing) come to you in abundance, so that you may always and under all circumstances and whatever the need be self-sufficient [possessing enough to require no aid or support and furnished in abundance for every good work and charitable donation].

Here, I learn that abundance is perpetual in nature. There is no such thing as shortage or running out. Abundance is richly furnished always, under all circumstances, regardless of the need. Abundance is the state of being self-sustained; connected to an inexhaustible source of supply. Abundance is a place where you draw on power that is beyond your natural ability, that causes you to see and operate beyond your current physical state of existence, "at all times, under all circumstances, regardless of the need." The more conscious you are of this state of being, the more it becomes your reality. Then, of course, the opposite it also true. As Jesus said, "all things are possible to him who believes," (or to those who have become highly developed in and conscious of his or her state of abundance in Christ (see Mark 9:23).

The literal meaning of the word *furnished* is "provided" or "equipped." In other words, whatever is needed has already been provided. As a Christian, it's assuring to know that God Himself has taken care to see that everything I need has been provided. Unfortunately, there are those who are not convinced of that provision. Negative circumstances and situations have caused them to think just the opposite. Instead of believing in abundance, they have placed their confidence and belief in the negative circumstances of lack.

The Place of Abundance: A Place of Obedience

The story of Elijah in 1 Kings 17 gives us a good picture of how abundance is attained.

> And Elijah the Tishbite, of the inhabitants of Gilead, said to Ahab, "*As* the Lord God of Israel lives, before whom I stand, there shall not be dew nor rain these years, except at my word." Then the word of the Lord came to him, saying, "Get away from here and turn eastward, and hide by the Brook Cherith, which flows into the Jordan. And it will be that you shall drink from the brook, and I have commanded the ravens to feed you there. (verses 1-4)

Notice, as Elijah held firmly to God's instruction for his life, complete provision would be available to him in spite of the conditions of drought that produced lack and insufficiency in his immediate natural environment. The place of abundance is always wherever God tells you to be. Your willingness to hear from God and obey Him will be critical in determining the level of the Father's abundance you will experience in life.

In verses 8-9 in the same chapter, we find that the "place of abundance" changes from Brook Cherith (place of covenant provision) to Zarephath (place of refinement). Often, the place of provision is shifted so that you may properly move into a place of growth, development, and refinement in your assignment. God does not want you to plateau and become comfortable and complacent. But every place God moves you, you will always find abundant provision for the assignment. When the brook suddenly dried up, the Lord still had a plan: "Then the word of the Lord came to him, saying, 'Arise, go to Zarephath, which *belongs* to Sidon, and dwell there. See, I have commanded a widow there to provide for you'" (verses 8-9). At two different times, God gave Elijah a word as to where he was to go. And both times, Elijah "remained in the place of abundance."

What we need, more than anything, is a word from God. Because no matter what dire circumstance we find ourselves in, anything short of a word from the Lord to sustain us is only a temporary fix. Provision is always temporary, brief, and fleeting whenever it does not come from God. The word God gives you may sometimes not make sense and may seem unlikely. But when you show up at the place God has directed you to be, your presence will transform the environment and make it conducive to the command He gave you. You become the key factor for transforming any environment or condition. When you show up is when things change.

The truth is, God commands your provision to be wherever He tells you to be. Elijah didn't have to wait to receive God's abundance. It was there before he showed up. Abundance is always there, despite what things look like. You've just got to know how to access it. If you're having trouble seeing your abundance, pray and ask God for revelation of it. There might be negative forces in your life, things like unforgiveness, bitterness or anger, that may be preventing you from seeing and receiving God's abundance. Be quick to repent, forgive, and love. There is no better place to be than "the place of abundance."

Abundance Is a Place of Faith and Order

We'll end this chapter by looking at abundance as a place of faith and order. It's a known fact that the manifestation of God's abundance is birthed through us as we desire it for the purpose of advancing the kingdom of God in the earth, meeting the needs of others.

Let's consider corporations and big businesses, for example. The greatest profit margins are enjoyed by those that tend to assess the trends, habits, and needs of the consumer. They examine the needs of the consumer and invest in strategies that meet those needs.

In the Kingdom, abundance comes when seed is planted in the direction of the need of humanity. Our investment is "seed" and our profit is "harvest." My pastor, Dr. Bill Winston, often states, eluding to Isaiah 48:17; "There is no such thing as a 'non-profit church' in the kingdom of God." Yes, or course, we have been categorized legally by the national tax agency as such, but we should never allow that categorization to distort our inner image where abundance is concerned. We do not rely on the world's system of buying and selling as the primary means of prospering. We are now engaged in sowing and reaping. The motivation is quite different in that our gains are not used to hoard, but rather to increase our capacity to receive more, distribute to others, and live up to the standard of redemption that Jesus died and payed with His blood for us to obtain (see 2 Corinthians 8:9, 9:6-10).

In John 6:1-13, Jesus demonstrated that when we shift our thinking to seed-based living as opposed to provision-based living, we are then able to live in the fullness of not only our own personal abundance, but in a place of abundance where we facilitate God's provision to the world. Jesus takes the seed of two fish and five loaves of bread, and with the harvest of that seed feeds five thousand men plus women and children who were in attendance that day as He taught them the Word of God. This He did to keep those gathered from having to travel a significant distance home and then buy and prepare food for their families and themselves. This was a gesture of kindness that also made receiving the Word that much easier.

The *place of abundance* can also be described as the point at which you simply obey the promptings of the Holy Spirit—what God is telling you to do. Notice, it was not until the disciples obeyed Jesus' instruction that they experienced supernatural abundance for the crowd gathered that day. They not only had enough, but they had more than enough! Where did it come from? It was already there. It had been provided before it was ever needed. Faith placed a demand on it as the Kingdom was sought by Jesus as He prayed to the Father and blessed the seed (two fish and five loaves of bread). This tells me that abundance is easily manifested with your seed and your faith.

There's much we can learn from this event, but one key point is this: Whenever you are ready to manifest abundance in and through your life, you will begin receiving instruction from God that will require faith and a seed. Your speech will change. Your actions will change. You will begin doing things and saying things in another manner. You will proceed as if what you are believing for has already manifested!

Someone who is receiving abundance never waits until manifestation comes to try and get ready for manifestation. You must function and operate at the level that you desire to receive. If you have a car that's 20 years old, and you're believing God for a new car, you must treat that 20-year-old car like it's a new car. Keep it clean! Get the junk out of the trunk. That's called putting action with your faith. You must operate at the level you desire to be.

Likewise, if you're believing God for increase in your finances, but you're not a tither, start tithing (Malachi 3:10). To get to the place of abundance, you must be willing to adhere to certain disciplines—some of which seem premature and out of order with where you are at the time. But that's God's way of preparing you to pursue a thing—to manage and develop the capacity to receive it. There is a place of abundance, and that place is the place of obedience and selflessness, and a place of faith and order.

Deuteronomy 8:18, *Amplified Bible, Classic Edition,* says, "But you shall [earnestly] remember the Lord your God, for it is He Who gives you power to get wealth, that He may establish His covenant which He swore to your fathers, as it is this day." God gives us all "power to get [abundance] wealth." But for us to walk in that place of abundance, for us to live like the Kingdom children we were created to be, we must do something. We must make sure we're in the right place—the place God has ordained us to be—at the time He has established for us to be there.

Abundance is waiting!

Chapter Nine

The Supernatural Nature of Abundance

Because God has promised us His best, there is an expectation on His part that we believe His Word, and that we receive what He has made available to us. Ephesians 3:20, the *Amplified Bible, Classic Edition*, says, "Now to Him Who, by (in consequence of) the [action of His] power that is at work within us, is able to [carry out His purpose and] do super-abundantly, far over and above all that we [dare] ask or think [infinitely beyond our highest prayers, desires, thoughts, hopes, or dreams]."

This passage supports the idea of God's desire for us to live an abundant life and never operate in lack. It also implies that God's ability to do for you is limited to your capacity for Him to do through you. In other words, "in consequence of the action of **His power that is at work within you.**" If His power is not at work within you then there should be no expectation for the "exceeding, abundant, and above" nature of God's abundance to flow through you. Why? Because there is no capacity built to receive it. I am convinced that oftentimes we pray and ask God for what we have no capacity to receive. God uses His very own power to do "exceeding abundantly above" (Romans 1:16) all that we can ask or think. He uses His power to make salvation available to us. He uses His power to bring about wholeness, wealth, prosperity—every form of provision—for us as His sons and daughters.

If you are meditating God's Word regularly, right now all these things are at work in you. There's no other way to expect to walk in God's blessing, or to live in His abundance than to have His Word in you. Remember Joshua 1:8, *The Message:* "And don't for a minute let this Book of The Revelation be out of mind. Ponder and meditate on it day and night, making sure you practice everything written in it. Then you'll get where you're going; then you'll succeed." The Word of God is your key, your blueprint to reaching your destiny and receiving God's abundance. You must have the Word, the Gospel of Jesus Christ, working in you. Like King David eludes to in the book of Psalms, you must hide God's Word in your heart as opposed to simply reading it. Just because you read the Word doesn't mean you believe it. Depositing God's Word in your heart, like planting a seed in the ground, is the evidence that you not only believe it, but that you trust and believe God to keep His Word.

Supernatural Abundance

God's abundance is supernatural! There's no other way to think of it. There's nothing we can ever do in the natural to enhance the manifestation of God's abundance except obey the Word of instruction He gives to us. Second Corinthians 9:8, *Amplified Bible, Classic Edition*, confirms that: **"And God is able to make all grace (every favor and earthly blessing) come to you in abundance,** so that you may always and under all circumstances and whatever the need be self-sufficient [possessing enough to require no aid or support and furnished in abundance for every good work and charitable donation]." **(emphasis mine)**

Abundance is God's doing and therefore it is supernatural. It defies need, insufficiency, and lack of all kind and under all circumstances. When under the influence of abundance-thinking, you have a disdain and disregard for the natural manifestations of lack and poverty. Your spirit will reject it without you consciously trying to do so. It's the same with sickness or disease. When your thoughts are saturated with health consciousness, sickness will annoy you. You want out of that sick condition or circumstance as quickly as possible because you know it is not of God and it is not for you. So, you apply the Word to that situation and before you know it, that sickness is gone. It's the same with anything where lack is concerned, whether it's a lack of peace, joy, love, friends, money, or health.

A key factor with God's supernatural abundance is the idea that its supply is perpetual, inexhaustible, and excessive in nature. It never runs out! You never hoard because there's always more. Every characterization of supernatural abundance speaks to the inexhaustible and the excessive—over-the-top, unlimited, boundless generosity of our heavenly Father toward His children.

Ephesians 3:8, *Amplified Bible, Classic Edition*, says, "To me, though I am the very least of all the saints (God's consecrated people), this grace (favor, privilege) was granted and graciously entrusted: to proclaim to the Gentiles the unending (boundless, fathomless, incalculable, and exhaustless) riches of Christ [wealth which no human being could have searched out]." It's important that we not think only of finances, but rather inclusive of finances, when we read this scripture. Wealth, you see, goes far beyond the scope of money. How about ideas? How about concepts or innovation? How about the fruit of the Spirit? What this scripture is referring to is a complete, comprehensive provision package that God has made available to each of us as believers.

God doesn't deal in shortages. He's a God of abundance, and that covers every area of our lives. Jesus said everything that belongs to His Father belongs to Him, and that He has revealed it to us (John 16:15). As believers, we have direct access to the nature of God and all that He has made available to us through Jesus Christ. Don't build a wall of theology that separates your thinking from the truth of God's best for your life. Make sure His Word is the basis of what you believe when it comes to receiving the supernatural abundance of God.

Dominating Time

Another supernatural aspect of abundance is that it will bypass and dominate time to get to you. Jesus' mother made a request for Him to create (not buy) more wine for the wedding celebration in which they had been invited. Here's Jesus' response in John 2:4, *Amplified Bible, Classic Edition*: "Jesus said to her, [Dear] woman, what is that to you and to Me? [What do we have in common? Leave it to Me.] My time (hour to act) has not yet come." In *The Message Version,* that verse says: "Is that any of our business, Mother—yours or mine? This isn't my time. Don't push me."

In other words, Jesus was simply telling Mary, "The Father hasn't released Me to do this kind of thing yet. The time has not yet arrived." Mary, in a sense, was operating beyond the order of time and had taken ownership of a need that required the domination of time. Her faith in the Father is obviously producing this dynamic outcome of abundance. She did not respond to Jesus' lecture on the matter regarding it not being the "right" time, so she proceeded to tell the servants to prepare to obey His next command (verse 5). Here's what happened next:

> Six stoneware water pots were there, used by the Jews for ritual washings. Each held twenty to thirty gallons. Jesus ordered the servants, "Fill the pots with water." And they filled them to the brim. "Now fill your pitchers and take

them to the host," Jesus said, and they did. When the host tasted the water that had become wine (he didn't know what had just happened but the servants, of course, knew), he called out to the bride-groom, "Everybody I know begins with their finest wines and after the guests have had their fill brings in the cheap stuff. But you've saved the best till now!" (verses 6-10, *The Message*)

Notice, no one had to plant grape seeds, attend to grape vines, harvest grapes, press grapes, nor process the grapes into wine. Here, we can be certain that several natural laws (including time) were bypassed in getting this supernatural abundance to Mary. Supernaturally, Jesus took it from water to wine instantly and it was delivered on demand! The supply was already there.

Who says it must take 25 years before you can see the vision that God has put in your heart come to pass? We subscribe to time as dictated by natural order. But time is a created thing of God that was placed in the same Earth in which He gave you dominion over. Once this is revealed to you, it can then be restored to you.

The Blessing Factor

The supernatural is that which can outperform the natural. Unfortunately, many Christians struggle in the natural to live supernaturally. This is impossible to do. The supernatural
is an embrace of the Blessing. We read before that Proverbs 10:22, *Amplified Bible, Classic Edition*, says, "The blessing of the Lord—it makes [truly] rich, and He adds no sorrow with it [neither does toiling increase it]."

The Blessing serves as an empowerment that leads to one's success and prosperity in life. When you received Christ, you received the Blessing. The Blessing is not any single thing. It's not a car, a house, or a big bank account.

The Blessing is God's literal empowerment on your life. It's His anointing and ability resting within you to be and do what you were created to be and do.

We have distorted and perverted the word *rich* so much so that most everyone equates it to money. The thing is, God has made us rich in many ways, including money. The word *rich* is defined as "abundantly supplied." A one-dimensional mindset regarding money will cause you to engage in un-healthy comparisons, and before you know it you are toiling to measure up to someone else's perceived success.

There is no such thing as improving on God's Blessing. It works independent of human effort by man, because it's supernatural. And because it's supernatural, it will produce supernatural abundance!

We will conclude this chapter with this idea: Deuteronomy 8:18, *Amplified Bible, Classic Edition*, says, "But you shall [earnestly] remember the Lord your God, for it is He Who gives you power to get wealth, that He may establish His covenant which He swore to your fathers, as it is this day." What is that power? It's God's enablement operating within you. It's the Blessing that comes to you (within you) when you surrender to Christ (the Anointing and the Anointed One). This is what God has given each of His children. With it, we have no choice but to thrive as we focus our attention on His plans and purposes for our lives (His kingdom).

Chapter Ten

The Law of Attraction

In this final chapter, I want to remind you that you became well capable of living in abundance (the best of God) the moment you received Christ into your life. Matthew 6:33, *The Message*, is proof of that. It says, "Steep your life in God-reality, God-initiative, God-provisions. Don't worry about missing out. You'll find all your everyday human concerns will be met."

In this translation, the word *steep* is used to suggest that our lives should be saturated in God's reality base for us. In God's reality, we are fully provided for. God desires His reality to become our reality. This happens as we direct our thoughts in the direction of His Word. God's reality is life as He would have it to be. It's living life the way He desires for you to live it, and not how you think you should, based on the world's reality—the world's way of doing and being right. The Bible is filled with God's expressed intent for you and I to live in abundance, success, and prosperity.

I don't want to conclude this writing without examining the Law of Attraction, and its relationship to you becoming more abundant-minded. The Word of God establishes through Scripture that you will attract into your life that which is imprinted upon your subconscious (Proverbs 23:7). In other words, with exact precision you become what you meditate. Your life will always produce the expression of what you think, see, and believe yourself to be. Life is truly lived from the inside out! The landscape or the surroundings of your life (both spiritual and physical) is created upon demand according to the blueprint within you. Even the conditions that were imposed on you must comply with the conditions living within you. It is the master plan of the

Father to ensure that no one possesses the key to your destiny without your explicit permission.

It is important that we possess the same image of ourselves that God has of us. This can only happen as we allow our minds to be renewed to His Word. I like how *The Message* translates Jeremiah 29:11. It says, "I know what I'm doing. I have it all planned out—plans to take care of you, not abandon you, plans to give you the future you hope for."

If it is our desire to live out God's intended plans for our lives, we must attract those plans to us. Let your mind and heart serve as a magnet to the literal persons, places, and things required to manifest the plans of God for your life. This happens when Jeremiah 29:11 is firmly placed in the deepest parts of your heart and mind. If your mind is not renewed to Jeremiah 29:11—if you're not thinking the way God thinks—then you will become tolerant to the conditions and circumstances that are contrary to His and that were never designed for you to live out.

Romans 12:2 talks about "proving" the good, acceptable, and perfect will of God. There is such a thing! This is a major reason for meditating the Word of God. It ensures proper navigation in life. You can literally avoid living in the wrong city, accepting the wrong job, or even marrying the wrong person for that matter.

David wrote in Psalm 119:11, *Amplified Bible, Classic Edition*, "Your word have I laid up in my heart, that I might not sin against You." The psalmist knew the importance of having God's Word living and working in his spirit. If you hold the Word in your heart, you will maintain a clear image of how God intends for you to live. Whenever you are tempted to conduct your affairs contrary to God's Word, the Word will conform you back toward the image of God within you. In addition, you will attract only that which is conducive to God's will for your life.

We've been pathetically conditioned by the world's system to see ourselves unlike God. The world attempts to constantly pervert our thinking away from the image of God and transform it into what the world desires to create within us. We look in the mirror and see white skin, black skin or brown skin, and our perception is that we are whatever society dictates that particular color, race or nationality to be. We look at how our nose is shaped, that we have slanted eyes, or that our hair is a certain color or texture and we think that is what defines us. No, that doesn't define you. God created you to be a spirit just like Himself. You are defined from the inside out. You are defined by what you believe and speak. You will attract into your life that which you have meditated, believed, and spoken.

Dominant Patterns of Thought

The law of attraction says, "I draw to myself that which I give my focus to—whether good or bad." If you focus on negative things such as offense, bigotry, unforgiveness, or the pains of injustice, then you'll attract more of the same in your life. When your thoughts are preoccupied with lack—not having enough, being poor, or having to work harder than necessary to have a decent life—then that lifestyle will continue to be an ongoing experience in your life. That's because your life circumstances have no choice but to obey the command of your most dominant pattern of thought. This is one of the greatest challenges for many people, including Christians. They spend a lifetime developing distorted images of themselves and others, and then they come to church and expect God to change their world for them—overnight. They give no regard to the process of meditation that is required to renew life from the inside out. They don't recognize that development of the mind is a requirement.

Living in God's kingdom is not automatic. Thoughts of lack and insufficiency are reinforced by strongholds that are established in the mind—strongholds that were created by the world's system. A stronghold is a fortified way of thinking (a mental wall). It represents your dominant pattern of thought. If your dominant pattern of thought is one of failure, then you will find that you will work hard to sabotage success while standing in defense of everything that reinforces failure. People will come to you with the right answers or solutions to your problems, but you won't recognize them as the truth. You will subconsciously fight against anything that will advocate or encourage your success. Whatever seems right to you becomes your reality.

When you decide to sit before God and be still, to receive His Word and allow it to minister to your inner man, the Word will give light to illuminate any and every situation you face. It will enable you to see the stumbling blocks well before they become obstacles in your path. It will reveal the tricks and traps of the enemy, so you recognize them and know exactly how to navigate around, over, or through them.

Say Something!

Mark 11:23-24 clearly represent the Law of Attraction. It says,
> For assuredly, I say to you, whoever says to this mountain, 'Be removed and be cast into the sea,' and does not doubt in his heart, but believes that those things he says will be done, he will have whatever he says. Therefore I say to you, whatever things you ask when you pray, believe that you receive *them*, and you will have *them*.

Notice that verse says, "Whosoever says...." The first thing you've got to do to attract God's will into your life is to "say" what He says. The reason most people do not see abundance is because they are not speaking abundance. You see, speaking to your mountain of insufficiency and lack is critical. But what you say to the mountain is just as critical. Jesus said if you say to the mountain to "Be removed and be cast into the sea...." You must speak in terms of "desired outcomes," not in terms of "current conditions."

Jesus said in John 6:63, "The words that I speak to you, are spirit, and *they* are life." The universe is subject to words. As a spirit being, your words are also spirit, and they are life. That means whatever you speak will manifest in one form or another. Why? Because words spoken and believed possess the capacity to create. It doesn't matter what the conditions may be. Your words can even target inanimate objects. Jesus gave clear examples of this throughout His time on the Earth, where He spoke to such things as a hurricane and a fig tree. That's how I live my life. I don't allow natural things or conditions to control my life. I have spoken to my car at times when it was acting crazy and said, "You will last until I decide to buy another car. When I decide to buy another car, then I'll let you go." Before long that car is working better than it did before. On one occasion, it even repaired itself while sitting inside a certified mechanic's shop. There was an explosion of some sort that happened in my engine. Something had blown up and there was coolant all over the ground underneath the car. I had the car taken to the shop, and when the mechanic checked it out, he said the car had blown a head gasket. Not really knowing what that meant, I asked and was told I would either need to repair the engine or buy another car. The cost to repair the engine was about $6,000 to $7,000. So, I told the mechanic to fix the engine.

A day or so later, I received a call from the mechanic saying the strangest thing had happened. When he pulled off the valve cover from the engine, the head gasket had somehow resealed itself. He said he would not have to replace the engine. "Well, put the cover back on, close it up and give me my car," I told him. More than five years later, that gasket remained sealed, and the car continued to run fine with more than 200,000 miles on the German-made engine.

What am I saying? Jesus said we can say to the mountain, "Be removed, and be cast into the sea." And as long as we don't doubt what we say, as long as we have faith in God and His Word, we can believe we have what we say, and receive it. The key is believing what we say and not allowing doubt to come in and rob us of God's best for us—His abundance. That's the Law of Attraction, and how you get things in life. They come from the inside out. Doubt and unbelief will push your desired outcomes far from you.

Paul, the Apostle, said whenever you have thoughts of doubt, you hold those thoughts captive and cast them down: "Casting down arguments and every high thing that exalts itself against the knowledge of God, bringing every thought into captivity to the obedience of Christ," (2 Corinthians 10:5). How do you do that? You do it with the Word of God. When the devil confronts you with negative thoughts, you don't just sit idly by and allow him to play with your mind. You don't sit back and say things like, "Well, you know, God is good and He's more than able to fight my battles." Yes, that's true. But that's not how God expects for you to handle the attack of the enemy. He expects you to exercise the power and authority He's given you to resist the devil and watch him flee. He expects you to go into counterattack mode—to begin speaking words that counter the negative thoughts the devil attempts to plant in your mind. You take those negative thoughts by the neck and cast them down no matter how long it takes. If they come at you 100 times in one hour, then that's how many times you cast them down.

The problem is, that's what most people don't do. They take a stand for a while, but when things start to get tough and they begin to feel seemingly overwhelmed, instead of continuing to fight and resist the devil, using the Word as their armor, they eventually get tired and give in to a false reality.

Here's the good news: The Word is designed to create God's reality and attract its outcomes into your life. When you're speaking the Word, you're not moving Heaven. Heaven has already moved on your behalf. What you're doing is conforming your spirit to attract the Father's already existing plan into the landscape of your life. You're making your spirit ready to receive all that Heaven has already done for you. When Jesus spoke the words, "It is finished!" while hanging on the cross, He wasn't referring to His impending physical death. He was talking about everything He had come to fulfill. He was talking about the life of abundance that His presence in the Earth made available to all mankind (see John 10:10; 1 John 3:8). The reality is, everything God is going to do for you has already been done. It's already completed! Your abundance is already packaged and ready for you!

Take It, It's Yours!

I want to conclude with an illustration that I believe will give you a clear picture of all that we've been talking about. I believe this is one of the most powerful examples of God's faithfulness to His children by providing for us in abundance, by giving us everything that we need, and ever will need. It's also a picture of how we so very often fail to recognize God's abundant provision.

As the story goes, a young Irishman sought to purchase a boat ticket to America, where he had hoped to immigrate. From his years of savings, the young man discovered he had enough money to pay for his ticket, but not enough to cover his meals while aboard the ship. Determined to seek the opportunity for a new life, he booked his passage, and then managed to pull together enough additional money to buy cheese and bread to eat while on his long journey.

One evening during the first two weeks at sea, the ship's captain was walking the deck when he noticed the Irishman sitting near the bow eating his cheese and bread. "Why aren't you in the galley eating supper with the other passengers?" the captain asked.

Sheepishly, the Irishman replied, "I regret sir that I only had sufficient funds to buy passage, but not enough to pay for meals." Surprised at the response, the captain looked at the man curiously and said, "Son, didn't you know that when you bought the ticket that your meals were included with the fare?"

Just as the Irishman didn't realize the true benefit of the ticket he had purchased, so are many Christians unaware of the true power behind God's intent for abundance in their lives. And because they don't fully understand it, they deny themselves the privilege of enjoying all that God has provided and fully outlined in His Word.

The Bible says in Hebrews 4:12 the Word of God is living and powerful, and sharper than any two-edged sword, piercing even to the division of soul and spirit, and of joints and marrow, and is a discerner of the thoughts and intents of the heart." Yet so many times people treat the Bible like any other book. They pick it up, read a few words and put it down— never really realizing the power contained in those pages. They may acknowledge the Bible is the Word of God, but I'm talking about truly realizing the power and the potential contained within the Word. And because they don't, like the Irish traveler, they miss out on everything God has provided for them.

God desired to bless Abraham so that he could be a blessing to others. And the same is true for you and I today. It's not hard to receive this truth if you will train your heart to believe it. Receive His abundance so that you can live the life He intended for you!

Prayer of Salvation

The Father's plan of Salvation through Christ is a decision on your part to yield to His Lordship in your life. The following prayer is the biblical basis for such a quality decision (Romans 10:9-10). After praying this prayer, it is imperative that you allow the Father to lead you to a "bible-teaching" church that believes in the ministry of the Holy Spirit. If you will get involved and connected in that church, you will grow and flourish (Psalms 92:13). Pray this prayer:

"Dear Lord, I come to You now just as I am. You know my life and how I have lived. Thank You for forgiving me as I repent of my sins. I believe that Jesus Christ is the Son of God, and that he died for my sins and was the Resurrection for my redemption. Now, I yield to You. Live Your life through me. I receive the gift of Your Holy Spirit. From this day forward I belong You! In Jesus' Name, Amen!"

www.ingramcontent.com/pod-product-compliance
Lightning Source LLC
Chambersburg PA
CBHW052111070526
44584CB00017B/2444